MAKING
MUSICAL INSTRUMENTS
WITH KIDS

67 Easy Projects for Adults

Working with Children

A Book and Audio CD
by Bart Hopkin

Hopkin, Bart, 1952-
    Making musical instruments with kids : 67 easy projects
for adults working with children / Bart Hopkin. -- Tucson,
Ariz. : See Sharp Press, 2009.
128 p. : ill. ; 28 cm. + 1 audio CD.
ISBN: 9781884365485

Summary: This is a book of easy-to-build, low-or-no-cost
musical instruments that can be constructed by children under
adult supervision, or, in some cases, by older kids without
supervision. Examples of the instruments include washtub bass,
driftwood marimba, thumb piano, bucket drums, and
flowerpot bells: simple stuff, but stuff kids can have fun with.

1. Musical instruments -- Construction. 2. Musical
instruments -- Construction -- Juvenile literature.

                784.1923

Cover design by Kay Sather

TABLE OF CONTENTS

ACKNOWLEDGMENTS

Several people read the manuscript for this book prior to publication, and their comments and suggestions have made this a far better book than it would otherwise have been. Among them, John Bertles, Robin Goodfellow and Katie Harlow — all of them experts with loads of hands-on experience in instrument making with children — gave most generously of their time and energy to help shape this book. My editor at See Sharp Press, Chaz Bufe, has been invaluable. His skill with the written word coupled with his knowledge of music make him the perfect overseer of a project such as this. Many more people — too many to name — have unknowingly contributed to this book by freely sharing with me their ideas about musical instrument making over the course of many years in this field. To all of these people, my sincere thanks.

— BH

INTRODUCTION

This book describes musical instruments simple enough for children to make. It is not written primarily for children though, but for adults who work with children. That includes parents, teachers, and others involved in the lives of young people. It's also for older kids who can read and follow the instructions, and for grown-ups who'd like to have a little musical fun themselves. In the classroom and out, instrument-making is a hands-on learning activity, and this book will serve well as an instructional resource in that activity. But most importantly, this book is a guide to simple, enjoyable instrument-making for its own sake.

Here's the promise I made to myself when I decided to create this collection of children's instruments:

  * that the instruments included should
      be simple and kid-buildable,
      use available and affordable materials,
      require no specialized or dangerous tools;

  * and at the same time the instruments should be
      playable by children, and
      good sounding

Simple to make plus good sounding, it turns out, is an elusive combination … but not an impossible one.

Over the years, many children's instrument-making books have been published. There are also a lot of resources on the world wide web. I've reviewed as much of this literature as I could get my hands on, and I've brought the best of its collective wisdom to this book.

The simplest of the instrument plans in this book are suit-able for preschool children, and the range of appropriate instruments extends through the primary and middle school years, and beyond. Many of the projects appear in both simple and more sophisticated forms, appropriate for kids of different ages and abilities. Younger children will be able to construct many of the more advanced projects if an adult performs just one or two of the steps — for instance, pre-cutting a two-by-four with a handsaw.

The majority of the instruments use commonplace, low-cost, widely available materials. (In a few cases I've suggested more specialized materials.) For instruments made from throw-aways, it helps to start gathering the needed items in advance. Candidates for collecting include tin cans, plastic tubs such as margarine or yogurt containers, jars, bottles, corks, cardboard tubes, chopsticks, and various styrofoam forms.

Tuning is an open question with children's instruments. You and your kids can have a wonderful time with random-pitch instruments, or with instruments that approximate standard scales only roughly. On the other hand, many of the instruments in this book are tunable, so there are good possibilities for those who wish to make tuned instruments as well. If that's one of your interests, be sure to read the chapter devoted to tuning (page 107).

For ideas on putting the instruments to use after you and your youngsters have made them, turn to the chapter starting on page 111.

Remember, too, to enjoy the sounds of the instruments on the accompanying CD.

Ready? Turn the page to begin.

TOOLS

Many of the instruments in this book require no tools at all. Others require commonplace implements like scissors and rulers. A smaller number require common hand tools like a saw, screwdriver or hammer, and just a couple of the most advanced plans call for an electric drill (the least scary of power tools). Here are some suggestions.

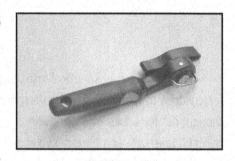

A lift-off can opener
This can opener pops off can lids without leaving sharp edges.

Lift-off can opener: There's a type of can opener that lifts the can lid off rather than cuts it out. It is safer and gives a more elegant-looking result than the old-fashioned kind. You can use the popped-off lids for various purposes, or even put the lid back on the can for neat temporary closure. The lift-off can opener is less widely available and more expensive than the ordinary type, but is worthwhile for projects with children. The Good Cook brand Monarch Series "safe cut technology" can opener from Bradshaw International is one model.

Work table, vises and clamps: For instruments requiring cutting, having a vise to hold the work piece makes work with hand tools a lot easier and safer. For not too much money you can purchase a small vise which clamps to a table. Often a C-clamp can serve the same purpose.

Hacksaw and carpenter's saw
The hacksaw (above) is easiest for children, and can handle most small jobs.

Saws: Hacksaws are the most kid friendly of saws. They're relatively small, light and sturdy. The small teeth are unlikely to accidentally cut anyone and the blade is less likely than those of larger saws to catch and bind mid-stroke. For most of the projects in this book that require a saw, a hacksaw will do. Securing the work with a clamp or vise will make sawing easier for children.

Tubing cutter: Some instruments in this book use plastic or metal tubing. There is a type of tubing cutter that works by means of a cutting wheel, hand-operated in a rotary motion. It cuts plastic or metal tubing without creating dust or fumes. When it comes to making tubing instruments more manageable for kids, this easy-to-use tool is a great help. Once again, securing the work with a vise or clamp makes the cutting much easier.

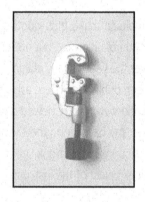

Tubing Cutter
To cut tubing, place the tubing cutter around the tube at the cutting location, and gently tighten down the cutting wheel. Rotate the cutter around the tube, further tightening the wheel bit by bit, until the tube is cut.

Adhesives: Common nontoxic household adhesives will do for the projects in this book. In addition to the familiar white glue (Elmer's Glue and other brands), I have found a product called Mod Podge, available at crafts stores, to be particularly effective for certain jobs. In cases where an adult can do the gluing, hot glue from a glue gun is often the quickest and easiest choice, because it's not messy and sets in just a couple of minutes. Hot glue guns are not expensive and are widely available at crafts stores, art supply stores, and hardware stores.

TIN CAN SET

If you strike the bottom of a tin can with a pencil or a chop stick, the sound you get may not seem very musical at first. But when you gather a set of cans and start playing rhythms and melodies — surprise! The tone takes on an unexpectedly appealing character.

Two plans for musical can sets are given here: a randomly tuned version, and a more advanced version that can be deliberately tuned.

TIN CANS — Simple Version

MATERIALS

Clean, empty tin cans in various sizes, at least 6 or 8 of them (more is better). The top should be removed with the bottom still in place. If possible, use the lift-off style can opener to open the cans (see page 2). Otherwise, carefully check the opened end of the can for spurs or jags, and dispose of cut-off lids out of the reach of children.

A towel or similar thick cloth, hand towel size or bigger.

Two unsharpened pencils, chopsticks or similar lightweight sticks to use as beaters.

TOOLS

None.

For more on mallets & beaters: see pages 104–106.

PROCEDURE

Optional: remove the paper from the cans.

Lay the towel out on a table, and place the cans open-end-down on the towel.

Strike the ends of the cans with the pencils or chopsticks. Select a set of them whose tones seem to complement one another nicely. Arrange those cans on the towel from lowest pitch to highest, or in any other sequence you like.

With small children, the selection process can be quite random; they may simply decide to include all the cans. Older kids may give more thought

For more on choosing among random-pitch sounds, see page 108.

to the process of selecting which cans to include in the instrument, looking for the cans that have the best sound and whose pitches go well together.

PLAYING THE TIN CANS

Strike the ends of the cans with chopstics or unsharpened pencils to play rhythms and melodies. When striking, let the stick bounce off, leaving the lid free to vibrate. If you use unsharpened pencils as beaters, you can get different tone qualities depending on whether you strike with the wood end or the eraser end.

TIN CANS — Advanced Version

The advanced version of this instrument is the same as the simple version, except that the cans can be tuned. You can use this tuning method if you don't need to tune to a certain scale, but would like to be able to tweak the tuning of the can's notes to suit your taste. You can also use it if there's a certain scale you want to tune to, such as the C major or C pentatonic scale that several of the other instruments in this book are tuned to, as discussed on page 108.

MATERIALS

Same as simple version above, plus ...

Adhesive putty or poster putty. Available at stationary stores, pharmacies, etc. Well known brands include Blu-tack, Sticky-tack and Scotch Adhesive Putty.

TOOLS

Hammer.

PROCEDURE

Gather and select your cans as described in the previous plan. Then tune them to whatever scale appeals to you using the following procedures.

To raise the pitch of a can: press downward firmly on the top of the can with an unsharpened pencil, chopstick or other implement, forcing it inward a tiny bit. Hit the can to hear the new note. It should be just a little higher than it was. Does it match the note you want, or is it still too low? If too low, tap the center very lightly with a hammer, denting the metal inward very slightly. Too much pressing or tapping may kill the tone. In that case, try again with another can whose natural tone is closer to the intended pitch.

For more on scales & tunings, see pages 107–110.

To lower the pitch of a can: Press a very small glob of adhesive putty onto the center of the lid, squashing it out and mak-

ing sure it's well stuck. Check the tone. Is it low enough now? If not, make the glob a tiny bit larger. If this process ruins the tone of the can, remove the putty and try again or switch to a new can.

Once the cans are tuned, lay them out on a towel for playing.

PLAYING THE TUNED CAN SET

Same as the simple version (see above).

ANY POTENTIAL DIFFICULTIES?

Struck cans tend to have a lot of strange overtones. This can make it difficult to get a clear sense of pitch from the cans, and sometimes they may seem to have dual pitch or no pitch at all. That's why it's good to have plenty of cans so you can choose the ones that sound best and put aside any that aren't so good. But remember that the slightly crazy tone quality of the cans is part of their character and charm.

The strange overtones can make the tuning process difficult, especially for perfectionists. My advice is, don't be a perfectionist.

Children doing the advanced version of the plan will have to be reminded to go easy with the hammer — very light tapping is enough.

FURTHER POSSIBILITIES

Children like instruments they can carry around. You can make a tin can set portable by strapping several cans together with strong rubber bands. (The common 3½" x ¼" rubber bands, referred to as size #64, are good.) To make the strapping easy, do it in sequence: first put a rubber band around two of them, then add a third, then and a fourth. The maximum you can hold in a group without slippage is about five. To increase stability, use two or more rub-

ber bands. The player can hold the set with one hand while striking with a pencil or chopstick in the other.

ACOUSTICS NOTES

How does the tuning work? When you strike the can-top with a pencil or chopstick, you make it vibrate. The stiffer the top is, the faster it vibrates, making a higher note. Pressing or tapping it in the center with the hammer bends it a little bit, giving it a slightly curved shape. This shape is stiffer than a flat lid would be. This makes it vibrate faster to produce a higher note. As for lowering th pitch: the heavier the top is, the slower it vibrates, making a lower note. Adding putty to the center makes it a little heavier, giving this result.

The tin can's overtones are usually inharmonic, which is a fancy way of saying that the overtones don't have a coherent musical relationship to the main tone that you hear. The cans that don't sound as good are often the ones in which the overtones are too loud and incoherent. Even in the ones that sound good, it's the inharmonic overtones that give them their peculiar tone quality.

FLOWER POT BELLS

Flower pot bells are simple to make and play, and a set of several pots with different pitches can sound lovely.

Clay flower pots can be hung upside down and played like other bells, but they work almost as well placed in the usual upright position and struck near the rim. A few pots of different sizes make a very pleasant (but limited) instrument. A larger number provides a more complete scale. As with the cans on page 3, there's an element of chance here: your scale will be made up of the notes you happen to find among the pots you have available.

There are many sorts of flower pots. Some of them are fancy and costly, but the common reddish earthenware ones are fine for musical purposes. If you don't have a good selection of these around your home already, you can buy them quite inexpensively in garden centers or variety stores. At the store, if you're gentle about it, you can tap the sides of different pots to see which ones make the nicest notes and which sound best together.

SKILL LEVEL

Provided with a selection of clay flower pots, even very small children can make this instrument.

MATERIALS

Flower pots in varying sizes.

Two unsharpened pencils, chopsticks or similar lightweight sticks to use as beaters.

TOOLS

None.

For more on mallets & beaters: see pages 104–106.

PROCEDURE

Strike the various pots near the rim and select a set of flower pots whose tones complement one another nicely. With small children, the selection process can be quite random; they may simply decide to include all the pots. Older kids may give more thought to the process of selecting which pots to include in the instrument and which to put aside, looking for those that have the best sound and whose pitches go well together.

Arrange the selected pots on the ground, the floor, or a table for easy playing.

PLAYING THE FLOWER POT BELLS

Strike the pots near the rim with lightweight beaters such as chopsticks or unsharpened pencils. The playing motion should be sideways against the sides of the pots near the rim.

ANY POTENTIAL DIFFICULTIES?

No surprise: the pots break easily. Stick with lightweight beaters if you're not confident that your kids can play with restraint.

For more on choosing among random-pitch sounds, see page 108.

FURTHER POSSIBILITIES

Some adults have fallen in love with the sound of flower pots and created sets with complete scales. But it requires lots of searching, and some luck, to find pots with just the right pitches for all the required notes.

With mature players who can be trusted not to whack the pots hard, you can get a fuller sound by using heavier, medium-soft mallets. A good choice is wooden spoons with one or two layers of moleskin padding the striking surface (see page 104 for details). Strike with the side of the head of the spoon.

If you create a large set, you may wish to create a two-tier framework to position the pots for easy playing. In designing a frame, keep in mind that the pots can sound well as long as they're supported from the bottom, but anything in contact with the rim or side walls of the pots will damp the vibration.

ACOUSTIC NOTES

In bell forms such as this, the sides and rim vibrate, while the center or base does not. That's why you can rest the pots on their bottoms without hurting the tone.

Rubber-band box zithers are easy to assemble. They produce a quiet but clear tone, and they make a good project for small children.

The first of the projects below presents the idea in its simplest form. Following that, under "Further Possibilities," are ways that you can develop and improve the idea. Most of the improvements are simple, but they enhance the sound noticeably. Finally, there are two more plans for nicer versions of the instrument.

BOX ZITHER – Simple Version

PROCEDURE

Place several rubber bands around the box as shown in the photograph.

TO PLAY THE INSTRUMENT

Pluck the rubber band segments that stretch across the open top of the box.

You can enjoy the random scale of pitches that you created when you put the rubber bands in place, or adjust their tuning to your liking. To adjust the tuning, stretch and slide the rubber bands over the edge of the shoebox, varying the tension on the playing segment of the bands. Different tensions will give you different notes. Precision tuning is difficult, but you can make recognizable scales.

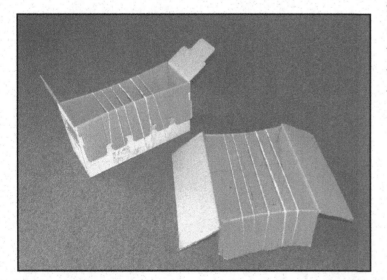

For more on scales & tunings, see pages 107–110.

Further Possibilities for Box Zithers

There are several things you can do to get better sounds out of the rubber bands and improve their range.

Using several different sizes of rubber bands allows you to get a wider range of pitches with clear tone quality. For large boxes, try extra-long seven-inch rubber bands. These are sold in office supply stores, sometimes under the name "file bands," and sometimes just as "long rubber bands."

With flat, ribbon-like rubber bands you can improve the sound by twisting them so that the playing segment takes on more of a round or spiral shape.

To keep the box from collapsing under the force of the rubber bands, reinforce it with a pair of rulers, unsharpened pencils, chopstick or other suitably sized sticks. Insert one on each side of the box under the rubber bands just below the edge of the box where they cross over.

You can make thicker rubber-band strings by twisting two or three rubber bands together and putting them on the box to function as a single string. These thicker strings give lower and fuller-sounding notes. The range of notes available on the instrument can be increased by having some single-band strings, some double-band strings, and some triple-band strings. If you do this you'll probably need to reinforce the sides of the box with rulers or pencils as described above.

You can also improve the sound of the instrument by making improvements to the box or using different kinds of boxes.

Larger boxes have the potential to create a louder and fuller sound than shoe boxes. With much larger boxes, use the extra-long seven-inch rubber bands.

Corrugated cardboard boxes are sturdier and often sound better than those made with a single layer of cardboard.

If the box has flaps for closing over the top, fold these down inside the box before putting the rubber bands on. In addition to getting the flaps out of the way, this makes the sides stronger.

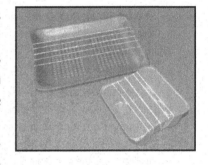

Small styrofoam containers can serve in place of boxes. Fresh mushrooms are often sold in styrofoam containers which, despite their small size, work nicely. Be sure to wash these containers well before use with children. Avoid styrofoam meat trays.

Thicker, more permanent boxes and bowls made of ceramic, plastic or metal are stronger, but they usually don't sound as good with rubber band strings as cardboard or styrofoam.

BOX ZITHER with soundboard and bridges

In this version of the box zither, the lid of the box serves as the soundboard. To raise the rubber bands up from the surface, two felt-tip markers are used as bridges. This set-up often sounds better than the open-top versions described above and is only a bit more complicated to make.

PROCEDURE

Stretch two rubber bands around the box.

Slip a marker under the rubber bands and slide it toward one end of the box as shown in the photo. Optionally, add another marker at the opposite end.

Add a few more rubber bands.

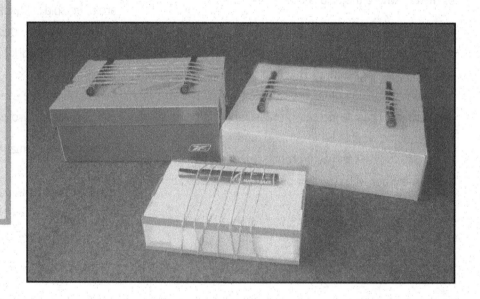

TO PLAY THE INSTRUMENT

Pluck the rubber bands.

You can enjoy the random tuning of the instrument, or tune deliberately. To adjust the tuning, stretch and slide the rubber bands to varying degrees over the edge of the box, varying the tension on the playing segment of the bands.

BOX ZITHER – Nine-String Deluxe Version

PROCEDURE

Remove the lid from the cooler. (Perhaps you can use it later to make another instrument.)

Place three seven-inch rubber bands longways around the styrofoam cooler, spaced about an inch apart.

Place a ruler under the rubber bands on each side, positioned so that it rides just about a quarter inch above the rim of the cooler.

Take two seven-inch rubber bands and twist them together, so that they are like a single extra-thick rubber band, still in loop form. Keeping them twisted as one, place this dual band on the cooler, passing over the rulers, alongside the file bands already there. Do this twice more, so that you now have three of the extra-thick strings.

Do the same again, but this time twist three rubber bands together. Place this triple-thick string on the picnic cooler alongside the others. Repeat this twice more.

You now have nine strings on your styro-zither – three single-strands, three double-strands and three triple. Your rulers have probably gotten out of position, so readjust them so that they are once again holding the strings just above the styrofoam rim. They should be just high enough to keep the rubber-band-strings from rattling against the rim of the styrofoam when plucked.

For more on scales & tunings, see pages 107–110.

MATERIALS

Styrofoam picnic cooler or similarly shaped Styrofoam container; any size will do. For environmental reasons, find a used one if you can or, better, intercept a suitably shaped piece of packaging styrofoam on its way to the landfill.

Seven-inch rubber bands. Available at office supply stores, sometimes under the name "file bands."

Two rulers or similarly shaped sticks.

TOOLS

None.

PLAYING THE DELUXE BOX ZITHER

Pluck the strings.

You can enjoy a random tuning, or deliberately tune the strings to your liking. Tuning, as with the simpler versions, is done by stretching and sliding the rubber-band-strings to varying degrees over the sides of the cooler to alter the tension on the playing segments. The thicker strings should be used for lower notes. You can tune this instrument fairly accurately, and if you don't pluck too hard the tuning will hold fairly well. As with any string instrument, you'll have to retune occasionally.

ANY POTENTIAL DIFFICULTIES?

The rubber bands don't last forever, but depending on tension they will hold for two weeks or more. (They deteriorate faster when they're left under high tension and exposed to light and air.)

An allergic reaction to latex appears in a small percentage of the population. This may be a concern when using rubber bands.

ACOUSTIC NOTES

Musical strings are not very good sound-makers if they're not attached to a soundboard. Being so slender, they have very little surface area. As a result, they don't do a good job of pushing the air around them when they vibrate, and their vibration scarcely makes its way out into the atmosphere for our ears to hear. But if you give a string a soundboard, the vibration of the string will cause the soundboard to vibrate too. With its greater surface area, the soundboard does a good job of transmitting the vibration to the air. Open box zithers don't have a soundboard under the strings in the way that other string instruments do, but the box as a whole acts as a soundboard, picking up the vibration from the string and providing the needed surface area for good projection.

CLAVES

MATERIALS

~ Either ~

Wood dowel, at least 16" long, between ¾" and 1¼" in diameter. Hardwood doweling is better than softwood, but even a softwood dowel can produce a decent sound. Available at hardware stores and lumber yards. Alternatively, try an old broom handle.

~ or ~

Bamboo, between about ¾" and 1½" in diameter, at least 16" long. Available at plant nurseries, garden supply stores, or perhaps in a neighbor's back yard.

TOOLS

Carpenter's saw or hacksaw.

Sandpaper.

Bench vise or C-clamp to hold the dowel during cutting. This will make the task easier for children.

Claves are nothing more than a pair of sticks, typically about an inch in diameter and eight inches long. The trick with claves is all in the playing technique: if you grasp one in each hand and hit the two of them together, as you'd naturally do if no one suggested otherwise, you get an unimpressive click. But if you hold them as described below, they give a brilliant, penetrating percussion tone.

SKILL LEVEL

This plan requires easy saw cuts with a hack saw or carpenter's saw.

PROCEDURE

Cut the dowel into two slightly unequal lengths, anywhere between six and nine inches long. (Shorter is better for thinner dowels and also for players with small hands.)

With sandpaper, clean up and slightly round over the newly cut edges. The easiest way for children to do this is to lay the sandpaper flat on a table, hold the paper with one hand, and use the other hand to draw the edges of the claves across the sandpaper.

PLAYING THE INSTRUMENT

Getting the playing technique right makes all the difference. For right-handers, cup one clave very lightly in your left hand in such a way that it rests loosely in the hand with a small air pocket formed underneath. In other words, grip it very lightly with your thumb and index fingers just above its halfway point, and its end resting lightly on the heel of your hand. This allows the clave to vibrate relatively freely when struck.

Several pairs of wood and bamboo claves

Hold the striking clave lightly between your right hand's thumb and index and middle fingers a half an inch to an inch below its center, with the end lightly touching the heel of your hand. This allows the striking clave to pivot when you strike the cupped clave.

Use the clave in your right hand to strike the middle of the cupped clave. The point of contact on the striking clave should be about an inch and a half from the exposed end. (Experiment to see where you get the best sound.)

It's the cupped clave, not the one used for striking, that produces the main tone. Since the two claves are slightly different lengths, you can get two different notes according to which one you hold in the cupped hand. Sometimes one tone or the other happens to fit the music better.

FURTHER EXPLORATION

If you have more doweling, you can make several claves in different lengths or thicknesses to get different tones.

ACOUSTIC NOTES

Acoustically, claves function much like the bars used in marimbas and other bar percussion instruments. In the sidebar on page 31 you'll find a discussion of how musical bars work.

CORRUGAPHONES

Here is a unique and enchanting instrument of a type that did not exist for earlier generations because the material it's made from — corrugated flex-tubing — did not exist. When air flows through corrugated tubing, bumping rapidly over the ridges in the tube wall, it creates a musical tone. A single tube can produce several different notes, depending on the air speed.

Corrugated tubes of small diameter — less than a half inch or so — can be sounded by blowing. Larger diameter tubes require more wind than lungs can provide. They can be sounded by whirling through the air. (Whirling causes air to rush through.) The plans in these pages, using corrugated plastic tubing, include both types: narrow tubes played by blowing, and thick tubes played by whirling.

SKILL LEVEL

Untuned Versions: For both the whirled and blown instruments, the untuned version can be made by anyone old enough to use good scissors.

Tuned versions: These require measuring.

To play the whirled corrugaphones, children need to be big enough to do the whirling, and responsible enough not to whirl where they may knock over a lamp. Fortunately the tubes are light in weight and not very dangerous.

MATERIALS

3/8" corrugated plastic flex tube. Plastic flex tubing is sometimes sold with a split down the side; be sure to get the unsplit variety. This size is sometimes hard to find, but it is available through Experimental Musical Instruments (www.windworld.com).

TOOLS

Scissors.

Measuring tape or yard stick (needed only for the tuned version).

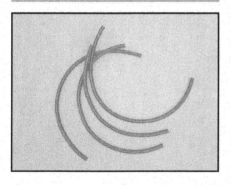

BLOWN CORRUGAPHONES

The sound of the blown corrugaphones is a whistling tone, delicate in the lower registers and shrill in the upper. They make rapid, cascading swirls of notes, reminiscent of bird calls.

A simple version of this instrument is nothing more than a single tube cut to a suitable length. For more variety, you can make two or more tubes cut to random lengths, or a tuned set cut to the lengths given below. Two or more tubes can be played one after another by a single player, or by a group of players each playing one tube.

PROCEDURE

Option 1. For a simple, single-tube instrument, use the scissors to cut a tube of about 20" (precise measurement isn't needed). This tube will produce a rainbow of tones depending on how hard you blow.

Option 2. For more variation, cut two or three tubes of different random lengths between about 16" and 24".

Option 3: For a nicely tuned set, try these four lengths:

23½" or 60cm	20½" or 52cm
17" or 43cm	15" or 38cm

Since each of the tubes actually produces several notes, these four lengths together provide a generous array of notes and musical patterns.

PLAYING THE BLOWN CORRUGAPHONES

The tube sounds with either blowing or sucking. The harder you blow or suck, the faster the air flows and the higher the tone. You can get rapid swirls of notes by shifting from soft to hard blowing or vice versa. With practice, you can play melodies by controlling the air speed.

For information on the group playing technique called "hocketing," see page 113.

WHIRLED CORRUGAPHONES

A single whirled corrugaphone tube can produce three or four different notes depending on the speed of whirling. The tone is an "oohing" sound, made richer by the directional effects of the whirling movement. It would be difficult to play familiar melodies with the whirlies, but the beauty of the sound and the choreographic nature of the playing give them an almost magical quality.

The simple version of this instrument is a single tube cut to a random length. For more variety of pitches you can cut two or three tubes.

(Labor-saving note: if you have made the side-struck flex tubes set described on pages 46-47, you've already made the instrument described here. Try whirling any of those tubes, particularly those in the middle length ranges.)

MATERIALS

Corrugated plastic flex tube, 1" in diameter or larger. One source for this material is the 1¼" corrugated plastic flex tubing sold in hardware stores as discharge hose for sump pumps. Other sorts of corrugated plastic tubing, sold for various purposes in hardware stores and elsewhere, will also work.

TOOLS

Scissors.

Measuring tape or yard stick (needed only for the tuned version).

PROCEDURE

Option 1: For a simple, single-tube version, use the scissors to cut a tube of about three or four feet long. If your tubing has any short sections without corrugations, avoid having these mid-tube, as the tubes will sound better without them.

Option 2: For more variation, cut two or three tubes of different random lengths between about three and five feet long.

Option 3: Cut four segments of tubing to the lengths given on the facing page. Measuring the tubes will be easier for a team of two rather than one person working alone, especially for the longer tubes. You don't need to be a perfectionist about getting the lengths exactly right.

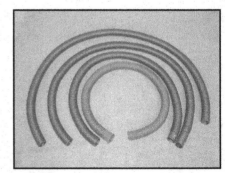

Tube number	Length	Pitches available
Tube 1:	62" or 157cm	G B D F G
Tube 2	57" or 145cm	(E) A C# E G A
Tube 3:	47" or 119cm	G C E G
Tube 4:	42½" or 108cm	A D F# A

PLAYING THE WHIRLED CORRUGAPHONES

Hold the tube at one end and whirl overhead or to the side. If the tube is too long to do this easily, whirl the last two feet or so of the tube while the rest remains stationary. The faster you whirl, the higher the note. With multiple players whirling tubes of different lengths, you can create compositions or improvisations by having different players whirl together or separately.

FURTHER POSSIBILITIES

For anyone who wants to add more notes to the whirled tube set, here are more lengths:

Length	Pitches available
53½" or 136cm	(F) Bb D F Bb
40" or 102cm	(Eb) Bb Eb G
35" or 89cm	(F) C F A

The notes you can get out of these tubes are all within a fairly narrow range. For ideas on broadening the range, read the Acoustic Notes below.

This kind of tubing can also work as side-struck tubing, played by percussion or scraping. See pages 46-47 for more on this.

ACOUSTIC NOTES

The notes available in any one tube don't form a complete scale. By working with two or more tubes of different lengths you can make more notes available to fill in the gaps in the scales. The set of four recommended tube lengths on this page creates a complete scale that way.

The notes that a corrugated tube can produce depend not only on length, but also on diameter. For that reason, cutting longer and longer tubes of the same diameter won't give you lower and lower notes. (It will give you different notes within the same general range.) To get lower notes you have to use larger diameters.

There are two ways you can make musical sound with bowls floating in water, and both are covered here. One works with metal bowls only:

Place the bowls floating upright on the water and play them as bells.

The other works with bowls of many materials:

Place the bowls upside down on the water with air trapped beneath, and strike from the side or above.

You can try each of these projects separately, or bring these two very different musical sounds together in the same pond or bathtub.

The bowl-bells are easiest so we'll start with them. After that we'll describe the inverted bowls, which are more interesting and unusual, and only a little more difficult to make.

FLOATING BOWL BELLS

You don't need to float a metal bowl in water for it to make a nice bell tone; just sitting on a table, most metal bowls will ring when you tap the side. But the floating bowl rocks when struck, and this imparts a lovely shimmer to the tone. If you add a small amount of water inside, this enhances the shimmering effect.

PROCEDURE

Place one or more bowls floating upright in water.
To tune to certain pitches, add water inside the bowls. The more water you add, the lower the pitch.

PLAYING THE FLOATING BELL BOWLS

Sound the bowls by striking the sides with your hand or, preferably, a moderately soft beater such as a superball beater.

For more on scales & tunings, see pages 107–110

MATERIALS

Metal bowls in various sizes. Any bowl that rings clearly when struck on the side will work. Stainless steel mixing bowls in different sizes are good.

Water to float the bowls in. For a single bowl, a large bucket or washtub will do. For more fun, float several bowls in a bathtub, kiddie pool, swimming pool or pond.

Optional: **soft mallet** such as a superball mallet. (The bowls can be sounded by tapping with bare hands, but the superball mallet will give a more pleasing sound and is easier for small children.)

For more on mallets & beaters, see pages 104–106.

TOOLS

None.

BOTTOMS-UP FLOATING BOWLS

Instruments of this type are sometimes called water drums. That name is also used for some other types of instruments, so to avoid confusion I'm calling them "bottoms-up floating bowls." The idea is to place several bowls of different sizes upside down on a water surface with air trapped beneath. Different-sized bowls yield different notes. The bottoms-up bowls are a random-pitch instrument, since tuning the bowls isn't practical. The tone is wonderful — deep and full.

The trapped air keeps the bowls afloat. However, they tend to tend to tip and sink sooner or later. To prevent this, the bowls in this plan have styrofoam floats.

PROCEDURE

If you're starting with a large piece of styrofoam, break it into 1" chunks. You don't have to be precise about this. If you're working with packaging foam that comes in smaller pieces to begin with, skip this step.

Use adhesive putty to attach the styrofoam pieces at regular intervals around the outside rims of your bowls as shown in the picture. (The putty won't hold the styrofoam on very strongly, but a very strong bond isn't required. The weak bond has the advantage that it allows for easy removal later.) With chunks of about one inch,

MATERIALS

Several bowls of different sizes. See notes on bowl selection below.

Styrofoam. You can use packaging "peanuts" or small chunks broken off from larger styrofoam pieces that would otherwise be headed for the landfill. Alternatively, corks may serve in place of styrofoam.

Adhesive putty (Blu Tack, Sticky Tack, and Scotch Adhesive Putty are common brands).

Water. Washtub, bathtub, watering trough, swimming pool or pond.

Optional: a **moderately soft beater** such as a superball beater.

More on choice of bowls:

The bowls can be of wood, plastic, metal or gourd. The best are usually fairly thin, yet still reasonably rigid. With wooden bowls, thin ones sound better than heavy, clunky ones. Plastic bowls work if they're sturdy, but thin-walled throwaway food storage bowls don't sound as good because they're too flimsy. Metal bowls often work well.

For more on mallets & beaters: see pages 104–106.

You can test to see which bowls work best by floating them upside down in the water and tapping them with your bare hand. (Prior to adding the styrofoam floats, most bowls float long enough for you to get a pretty good idea of the tone.)

TOOLS

None.

Bottoms-up Floating Bowls in water

eight chunks evenly spaced around the rim is good for most bowls. With the smaller packaging "peanuts," use more. Notice that the chunks don't go on top of the rim; they go around the outside. That way the bowl floats with the rim in the water, trapping the air inside.

Float the bowls, bottoms-up, on the water.

PLAYING THE INSTRUMENT

Strike the bowls with bare hands or with a soft beater. Try striking different parts of the bowls, top or sides, to see what brings out the best tone.

ANY POTENTIAL DIFFICULTIES ?

Either type of floating bowl could sink in deep water and be difficult to retrieve.

Remember to be sensibly cautious with children around water deep enough to fall into.

ACOUSTIC NOTES

Floating bowl bells produce their tone in the same way as other bells. The greatest vibration is near the rim, while the base scarcely vibrates. When you tune by adding water, the water slows down the vibration, making the pitch lower. The more water you add and the farther it rises up the sides of the bowl, the lower the pitch.

For the bottoms-up bowls, striking the bowl on the side or bottom excites a vibration in the enclosed air. This is transmitted to the water below, and the surface of the surrounding water transmits it to the air. Bigger bowls, enclosing more air, make lower notes.

The air sound is not the only sound in the bottoms-up bowls. The percussion sound from the bowl itself also contributes. If you listen carefully you may be able to recognize the two parts of the sound separately. This is particularly noticeable with metal bowls, because the high, ringing sound of the metal stands out from the lower tone of the air resonance. It's the air sound that is most beautiful, so it's best to play in ways that minimize the percussion sound of the bowl itself. For instance, using a hard beater would bring out a lot of bowl sound and not so much air sound, so a fairly soft beater is usually better. Striking on the bowl's rounded side rather than the flat top also helps.

RASPS

Almost anything with a ridged surface can be used as a rasp to produce scraping sounds. And as you can hear on the CD, the sound-world of scraping is more diverse and colorful than you might expect. On this page is a list of things that make good rasps. Since rasps need to be scraped with something, I've also included suggestions for things to use as scrapers.

COARSE RASPS

Objects with ridges between about an eighth of an inch and three eighths of an inch apart make characteristically rough sounds. They're usually scraped with a small, hard stick. Good candidates are:

Corrugated flex tubes of plastic or metal. You may have such tubes around the house left over from some purpose or other. Otherwise you can find them at hardware stores.

Broiler pans (the ridged drainer piece).

Old fashioned washboards.

Tin cans with ridges in the sides; also some kinds of plastic drinking cups and food take-out containers.

Corrugated cardboard (the flexible kind with the corrugations exposed).

Stair treading (various materials made to prevent slipping on stairs).

Scrapers for coarse rasps:

Chopsticks or unsharpened pencils.

Other small, hard sticks. They can be as short as 4 or 5 inches long.

A piece of stiff wire or thin metal rod. An especially effective type can be made from a piece of coat-hanger wire 16" long. Bend it double to make a dual-prong scraper 8" long. For safety, use pliers to loop a quarter inch on each end back on itself to round off the pokey ends.

Whisks (the wiry metal kitchen gadget used for stirring and whipping).

Silverware such as spoons (you can hold the spoon end and scrape with the handle).

FINE RASPS

Objects with ridges less than about an eighth of an inch apart make funny high-pitched sounds. Some candidates for fine rasps:

Long bolts or screws, as well as threaded rods. (Threaded rods are steel rods threaded like those on a bolt but much longer. They're available at hardware stores.)

Fresnel lenses. A Fresnel lens is a type of magnifying lens that has fine ridges in the surface. They are often made from inexpensive plastic. Fresnel lenses are available as surplus items from at www.sciplus.com.

Vinyl LP records. Children may not be familiar with these, but there are plenty still around that you might be able to intercept on their way to the junk heap. Just be sure not to scratch up someone's treasured old recording.

Hair combs.

Sandpaper. See the discussion below.

Scrapers for fine rasps:

A stiff card, playing-card size or bigger.

A plastic scraper. Use scissors to cut a card-like shape from a plastic fruit juice bottle or other stiff plastic material.

The special all-purpose scraper described at the end of this section.

Sometimes fingernails work.

PLAYING RASPS

Scraping sounds can be surprisingly interesting and versatile, and there's room for artistry in the playing. Try scraping fast and slow, as well as fast-to-slow and slow-to-fast. Try scraping with different kinds of scrapers and using different parts of the scraper.

Some rasps don't project their sound well; for example, hair combs. There are two ways to increase sound projection for combs and similarly quiet items. One is to hold the rasp against a surface that can serve as a soundboard, such as a table top or a cardboard box. The other is to scrape with something that itself has more surface area. Try a stiff playing card, a piece of aluminum flashing, or any similar thin, flat, semi-rigid object. The specially made scraper described on page 23 is particularly good for this purpose.

SANDPAPER

The swishy rhythmic sound of sandpaper scraping is perfectly suited for many kinds of music. Children's instruments books and websites often suggest making sand blocks. These are pieces of sandpaper stapled to wooden blocks for scraping together. But with the hard wooden backing, the two pieces of sand paper very quickly wear each other out, losing their grit and with it their tone. Also, the hard backing inhibits the vibration, diminishing the volume and sound quality.

I don't know of a way to keep sandpaper from wearing out, but

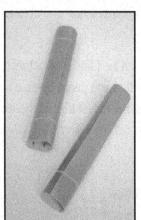

you can slow the wearing process and get a better sound by eliminating the wooden blocks and using the following approach.

PROCEDURE

Roll the two pieces of sandpaper into cylinders large enough that much of the sanding surface remains exposed.

Optional: Use rubber bands or tape near the ends to secure the cylinders so they don't uncoil.

PLAYING THE INSTRUMENT

Scrape the two sandpaper cylinders against one another. Try long, slow scrapes as well as fast, short scrapes. No need to press hard — a light stroke sounds just as good and creates less wear. When portions of the sanding surfaces begin to wear out, rotate the cylinders to scrape in different areas.

ALL PURPOSE SCRAPER

This gadget brings out great scraping sounds from almost any rough surface. Make two of them so you can use one in each hand.

PROCEDURE

Using scissors, cut two pieces from the flat sides of a plastic orange juice jug in the shape shown in the drawing.

Glue the plastic pieces to the bottoms of the cups, as shown in the photo.

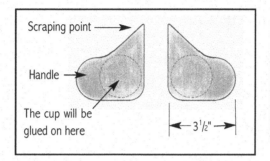

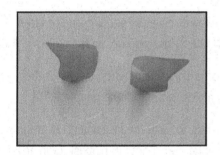

PLAYING THE ALL-PURPOSE SCRAPER

Hold the plastic pieces by the rounded part that sticks out to the side. Scrape the pointed tip against any of the rasps mentioned above, or against any other rough surface. The scraping sound will be loud and expressive.

Materials

An empty plastic orange juice jug, half gallon size, or other stiff plastic container (milk jugs are made of thinner plastic and aren't stiff enough).

Two large throwaway cups of styrofoam or thin plastic.

Glue. Hot glue works well and is quick. Alternatively, use a non-toxic crafts glue such as Mod Podge.

TOOLS

Scissors.

Glue gun (needed only if you use hot glue).

ACOUSTIC NOTES

When you scrape the pointed tip of this all-purpose scraper over a rough surface, the agitated movement of the tip is transmitted to the cup. With its larger surface area, the cup acts like a soundboard, projecting the sound into the air loud and clear.

PERCUSSION GLASSES & JARS

Most glasses, jars and bottles produce clear tones when struck on the side with a suitable beater. Glassware in different sizes and shapes give you different pitches. You can create a very appealing glass percussion instrument by gathering a lot of glasses and jars and selecting those that sound well together. For a more carefully tuned set, adjust the pitches by adding water: the more water, the lower the note.

SKILL LEVEL

Untuned version: This version of the glass percussion set, played with light beaters, is suitable for small children.

Tuned version: Making a tuned set requires a good ear and attentive listening, better suited for children over 11.

GLASS PERCUSSION SET, Simple Version (no water tuning)

MATERIALS

A selection of glass jars, bottles or glasses. The more you have on hand, and the more varied in size and shape, the better.

A towel.

A pair of chopsticks, unsharpened pencils, or similar lightweight sticks to use as beaters.

TOOLS

None.

For more on choosing among random-pitch sounds, see page 108.

PROCEDURE

Lay out a towel on a table or counter top. (The towel serves as padding and reduces unwanted noise.) Place the glasses, jars or bottles, right-side-up, on the towel.

Strike the sides of the jars with a chopstick or unsharpened pencil. Listen for their different tones. Most of the jars will produce a clear note. Pick the ones you like.

The littlest children can use these bottles or jars to form the instrument. Arrange the chosen jars in a row. Sequence them from the lowest note to highest, or in any other order you like.

Older kids can be more selective, especially if there are many pieces of glassware to choose from. Listen for the musical notes. Many of the notes will go well together, showing a pleasing musical relationship even if you don't know what scale they're forming. Choose the ones that sound best together to form the instrument.

PLAYING THE GLASS PERCUSSION SET

Strike the sides of the jars with the pencils or chopsticks to play rhythms and melodies. For a stronger sound, more mature kids who can be trusted not to hit too hard can use a heavier beater such as the handle of a spoon.

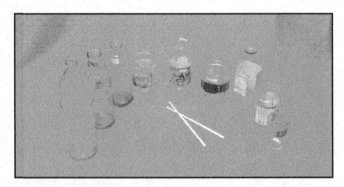

GLASS PERCUSSION SET, Advanced Version (with water tuning)

MATERIALS

A selection of bottles, jars and glasses.

A pair of chopsticks, unsharpened pencils or similar sticks for beaters.

A towel.

TOOLS

None.

PROCEDURE

Lay out a towel on a table or counter top. Place the glasses, jars or bottles, right-side-up, on the towel.

Begin checking their tone qualities and pitch relationships by striking the sides with a chopstick or unsharpened pencil. Put aside any that don't produce a clear tone.

With the remaining jars, think about making a scale as you listen to their various pitches. Perhaps some of your glasses or jars, taken together, suggest the beginnings of a scale. It might be a do-re-mi scale or some other scale that makes musical sense to your ears. When there's a note that you'd like to hear in your scale that none of the untuned jars provides, look for a jar whose note is a little higher than the desired note. Add some water to lower the pitch, check it again to see if it now produces the note. If not, continue adding water until you get it right.

For more on scales & tunings, see pages 107–110.

When you've got your tuned set, place them in a row for convenient playing. You can arrange them from the lowest note to highest, or in any other order you like.

PLAYING THE TUNED GLASS PERCUSSION SET

Same as with the simple version as described on page 24.

FURTHER POSSIBILITIES

Like glasses and jars, some types of bowls produce bell tones when side-struck, and can be water-tuned as well. Best are metal, glass and ceramic bowls. Bowls can be especially good for water-shifting shimmery effects. If you're interested in trying your luck with bowls, the instructions for the jars above should be enough to get you started.

ACOUSTIC NOTES

For information on how water-tuning works, see the acoustic notes for the floating bowl bells on page 18.

All you need to make a good shaker is a suitable container and some seeds or pebbles to put in it. Here are several ideas on how to do this.

BASIC SHAKER

PROCEDURE

Clean the container if necessary.

Place some shakable material inside the container. A small handful is usually about right for good shaking. If you put in too much, it will dampen the sound.

Replace the lid. (If your container is a can with the lid removed using a lift-off style can opener, use tape to fix the lid back on.)

PLAYING THE SHAKER

Shake it!

People with big enough hands and small enough shakers can create nice effects by cupping the shaker in two hands and opening and closing the hands while shaking.

ANY POTENTIAL DIFFICULTIES WITH THIS INSTRUMENT?

When you shake a shaker, there's a slight delay between the start of the motion and the sound, and following that there's an after-beat effect that comes when the motion stops. In situations where good timing is important, beginning shaker players tend to come in with their sounds behind the beat. Experienced percussionists play with a rolling motion that controls these effects.

MATERIALS

Small container made of hard material, with a lid that can be removed and replaced. Suggestions:

Small, hard plastic bottles, small glass jars, spice bottles, empty salt shakers, plastic easter eggs.
Also good: small tin cans (think of tuna fish cans) which have been opened using the kind of can opener that lifts the lid off rather than cutting it out (see the photo on page 2).

Shakable material to go inside. Suggestions:

Hard, dry beans; unpopped popcorn; pebbles, small hardware items such as nuts, washers, or ball bearings.
For a quieter, more swishy sound, try dry rice or barley.

TOOLS

None, unless you need a can opener (the lift-off type, described above).

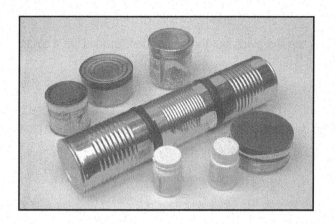

Various shakers, including simple shakers made from small tin cans, jars and plastic bottles. Also shown are a long shaker (three tin cans) and a drum shaker made of a tin can with a balloon membrane.

MATERIALS
for the long shaker

Three same-size tin cans (14-ounce soup-can size is good).

Shakeables to go inside: pebbles, dry popcorn or beans, etc. (See the longer list on in the materials list on page 26.)

Adhesive tape (cellophane tape, electrician's tape, or masking tape).

TOOLS

Can opener (preferably the lift-off kind; see the picture on page 2).

LONG SHAKER

This extra-long shaker allows a greater variety of sounds. It's made of three connected tin cans, and takes advantage of the ridges in the sides of the cans to enhance the sound as shakables slide over them.

PROCEDURE

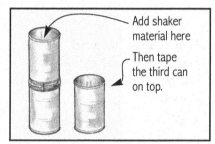

Add shaker material here

Then tape the third can on top.

On two of the cans remove only the tops; on the third remove both top and bottom. Clean the cans and remove their paper labels.

Tape the can that has top and bottom removed to one of the cans with only the top removed as shown in the drawing.

Add some shakables to the joined cans. Tape the third can to the other two.

PLAYING THE LONG SHAKER

Shake forward and back and side to side, or tip side to side. Different motions bring out different sounds.

DRUM-SHAKER

Instead of a lid, this shaker has a balloon membrane that acts like a drumhead, adding a new sound to the mix.

PROCEDURE

Place a small handful of shakeables in the container.

With scissors, snip off the neck part of the balloon.

MATERIALS
for the drum shaker

Container: a small jar (no lid needed) or a small can such as a tuna fish can with the lid removed.

Shakeables to go inside: pebbles, dry popcorn or beans, etc. (See the list in first shaker plan, page 26.)

Large balloon.

Rubber band.

TOOLS

Scissors.

Can opener (preferably the lift-off type), needed only if your container is a can.

Stretch the balloon over the top of the container like a drumhead. To keep it in place, put the rubber band around like a collar.

PLAYING THE DRUM SHAKER

Shake! Explore the different sounds of the container and the balloon drumhead. Try cupping one hand over the balloon part while shaking, opening and closing it over the balloon drumhead to bring out different sounds.

BALLOON SHAKER

This shaker produces a wonderful, deep drumming like distant thunder. When the light hits it right, you can see the silhouettes of the popcorn or dry beans dancing around inside, a wonderful visual effect. You can bat it around, playing with it like any balloon as it makes its sounds.

PROCEDURE

Add a small handful of unpopped popcorn or dry beans to the balloon, dropping them in bit by bit through the narrow neck.

Blow up and tie the balloon.

PLAYING THE BALLOON SHAKER: Shake it or bat it around in the air.

MATERIALS
for the balloon shaker

Large balloon or punch ball (a punch ball is an extra large, heavy balloon sold alongside the regular balloons at party stores).

Shakeables. Unpopped popcorn or dry beans.

TOOLS

None.

Thanks to Robin Goodfellow for the balloon shaker idea.

BAR PERCUSSION

Bar percussion instruments are instruments like marimbas and xylophones with sets of tuned bars played with mallets. The bars may be of wood, metal, or any other rigid material. They make excellent homemade instruments because they're easy to understand, easy to assemble, and they sound great.

Several bar percussion instruments appear on these pages, ranging from simple, untuned bar sets to more advanced instruments capable of serious music making.

FOUND-OBJECT BAR PERCUSSION

SKILL LEVEL

Laying the wrenches across the rope is easy enough for early grade school children. The cutting of the rope (if necessary) might call for an adult or older child.

MATERIALS

A set of box wrenches like those shown in the photo. A typical set would consist of about 10 wrenches in sizes ranging from ¼" to 1" (those numbers represent the size of the nut that the wrench is meant to fit). Many people have a set of these around the house. If not, you can purchase a set new at a hardware store or (less expensively) one of the discount tool catalogs online, such as Harbor Freight at www.harborfreight.com.

About three feet of rope. ¼" thick or thicker.

TOOLS

None, unless you need scissors to cut the rope.

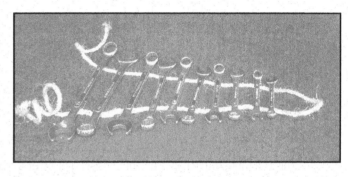

Almost any rigid object in the shape of a bar or stick or tube can function as a musical bar, given the right sort of mounting. For this plan I'll outline the procedure for making a random-pitch bar instrument from one suitable item, a graduated set of box wrenches like those shown in the photo.

PROCEDURE

Put aside one of the smaller wrenches to use as a beater. Lay the rope out and place the remaining wrenches across it in sequence from largest to smallest as shown in the photo. Because of the shape of the wrenches, the ideal support point will be closer than usual to the ends, with the wrenches crossing the ropes at about a sixth of the wrench-length from each end.

PLAYING THE WRENCHES

Strike the wrenches near the center with the beater wrench.

ANY POTENTIAL DIFFICULTIES?

Since the wrenches are not fixed in place, they'll tend to dance out of position when played. When this happens, just move them back in place and continue.

FURTHER POSSIBILITIES

Even if you don't make this particular instrument, it illustrates the idea that many commonplace objects are bar instruments waiting to happen. Here's another example: You can to make a melodic, random-scale instrument from pieces of scrap wood between about 8" and 24" long. For the cross-supports, try a pair of bath towels rolled up to form something like thick ropes. For the bars in the scrap-wood instrument to sound well, position each bar with between a fourth and a fifth of the length overhanging the towels at each end. Find a suitable beater, and strike near the center. The photo on the right shows another variation on this idea.

A scrap wood xylophone at the beach. Bars, cross supports and the mallets all are made of driftwwood.

BOLTS ON CUPS

This is a random-pitch instrument consisting of screws or bolts resting on styrofoam cups. The cups serve not only to support the bolts, but also to enhance the sound. The sound is a clear-pitched chiming tone.

This is a random-pitch instrument consisting of screws or bolts resting on styrofoam cups. The cups serve not only to support the bolts, but also to enhance the sound. The sound is a clear-pitched chiming tone.

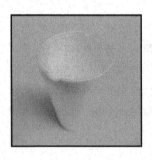

For more on choosing among random-pitch sounds, see page 106.

PROCEDURE

The bolts are placed across the tops of styrofoam cups as shown in the photo on the facing page, one bolt per cup. To keep the bolts from rolling off the sides of the cups, make small indentations in the rims of the cups at the points where the bolts are to pass over. Do this with fingernails, pinching away a shallow semicircle as shown in the photo on the left.

If you have plenty of bolts to choose from, look for those that have the nicest tone and which together give you the most appealing musical scale.

SKILL LEVEL

This instrument requires just a bit of manual dexterity to make and play. Recommended for ages 8 and up.

MATERIALS

Styrofoam drinking cups. Larger cups are better than smaller. You'll need several of them.

Bolts and/or large screws between 5" long and about 9" long. You'll want at least 4 or 5 of them in a variety of sizes and thicknesses. If you don't have a sufficient collection of such bolts around the house, pick them up at the hardware store.

One slightly smaller bolt or large nail to use as a beater.

TOOLS

None.

30

TO PLAY THE BOLTS ON CUPS

Strike the bolts at the center with a large nail or screw.

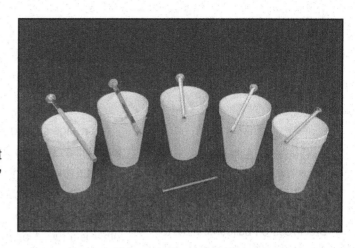

ANY POTENTIAL DIFFICULTIES?

The cups and bolts tip over fairly easily. If they do, just right them and resume playing. Also, see "Further Possibilities" below.

FURTHER POSSIBILITIES

Make this instrument more stable by gluing the base of the cups to a board using white glue, hot glue or other adhesive.

For a version of this instrument that is deliberately tuned to the scale of your choice, you can replace the bolts with sections of ¼" steel rod, tuned by ear by cutting to different lengths. See the "Rods on Balloons" plan on page 31 for ideas.

USEFUL INFORMATION FOR BAR PERCUSSION INSTRUMENTS

For percussion bars to work, the bars should be held in a way that leaves them free to vibrate. Whatever supports them must be padded or flexible, and the supports should be located where they'll have the least damping effect on the bar. In the most important pattern of vibration for the bars, there are two points of minimum vibration, and for minimum interference, these two points are the best places to locate the supports. Typically they're located between a fourth and a fifth (22%) of the bar length from each end.

A percussion bar's pitch depends on two factors:

1) Mass: the more weight the vibrating parts of the bar have, the slower it vibrates, making the pitch lower.

2) Rigidity: The stiffer the bar, the faster it vibrates, which makes the pitch higher.

That leads to these tuning rules:

To raise the pitch of a bar, shorten it. This reduces the amount of weight it has to throw around, making the pitch higher.

To lower the pitch of a bar, make the bar thinner at the middle. This makes it less rigid at the main flex-point, thus lowering the pitch. However, with some types of bars this kind of center-thinning is difficult to do. When that's the case, use the alternative below.

Alternative for lowering the pitch: Simply cut a new bar slightly longer. This is useful for tubes and any other materials which can't easily be thinned.

TWO BALLOON-MOUNTED METAL BAR INSTRUMENTS

SKILL LEVEL

Silverware on balloons: The hardest task is inflating and tying the balloons. If an adult handles that, the project is suitable for young children.

Steel rods on balloons: This is suitable for older children, ages 13 and up. The builder must measure and cut ¼" steel rods with a hack saw.

Sausage-shaped balloons can serve as supports for percussion bars. The balloons do a great job of bringing out the tone of the bars, especially for bars made of metal (the reasons why are explained under "Acoustic Notes" on page 34).

Two balloon-mounted bar instruments appear here. One is a random-pitch instrument suitable for younger children, with everyday silverware for the bars. The other is a tuned instrument suitable for older children, with bars made from steel rod that can be purchased at a hardware store.

Silverware on Balloons

PROCEDURE

Inflate two sausage-shaped balloons.

Place a strip of double-sided tape along the side of each one.

Place pieces of silverware across the two balloons resting on the double-sided tape as shown in the picture. With the balloon mounting, it's not crucial to have the correct amount of overhang.

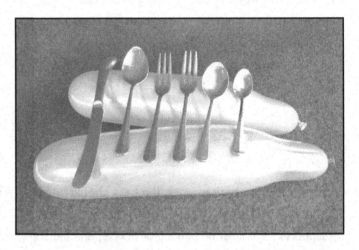

PLAYING THE SILVERWARE

For more on choosing among random-pitch sounds, see page 108.

Strike the silverware pieces near the center with felt tip pens or other beater. You can experiment with different scales by trying different pieces of silverware and selecting those that sound best together.

MATERIALS

Balloons, sausage-shaped or serpent-shaped. You need two, but it won't hurt to have extras.

Silverware. Try a random selection of different-sized spoons, forks and table knives (the dull kind).

Double-sided tape.

One or two beaters. Try a pair of large felt-tip pens or other medium-hard, medium light-weight beaters. A pair of small spoons works, but the tone is a bit harsh.

TOOLS

None.

For more on mallets & beaters: see pages 104–106.

MATERIALS

Balloons, sausage-shaped or serpent-shaped. You need two, but it won't hurt to have extras.

¼" steel rod, eight feet. Available at hardware stores.

Double-sided tape.

One or two beaters. Try a pair of large felt-tip pens or other medium-hard, medium light-weight beaters.

TOOLS

Hacksaw.

Vise or clamp to secure the rod while cutting.

Leather gloves for safety while cutting and filing.

File.

Tape measure or yardstick.

Felt tip marker (to mark off measurements).

A TECHNICAL NOTE FOR PLANS THAT INCLUDE STEEL TUBES OR RODS

This applies to the plans on this page and on pages 36-37.

If you cut tubes or rods to the lengths given in the plans, the resulting scale will be well tuned relative to itself. But there's a chance that it won't be perfectly in tune with other instruments tuned to the standard pitch of A=440. (This will happen if the rods or tubes you get aren't manufactured to the same specifications as the material that the author used to make the prototype instruments for the plans.)

If that happens but you want standard tuning, you can fine-tune using the tuning principles described in the "Useful Information" Sidebar on page 31.

Steel Rods on Balloons

PROCEDURE

Cut the rods to the lengths in the following chart. Use a hacksaw and secure the rods in a vice or clamp for cutting. Wear leather gloves to prevent any danger of cutting your hands on the end of the rod as you finish the cut.

Pitch	Length (Inches)	Length (cm)
C	13⅛"	33.4cm
D	12⅜"	31.5cm
E	11¹¹⁄₁₆"	29.7cm
G	10¾"	27.3cm
A	10⅛"	25.7cm
C	9⁵⁄₁₆"	23.6cm
D	8¾"	22.3cm
E	8¼"	21.0cm

Smooth over the newly cut ends of the rods with a file. The easiest way to do this is to hold the file flat on a table and draw the newly cut ends across the file to round off the edges.

Inflate two balloons.

Place a strip of double-sided tape over the length of the side of each balloon.

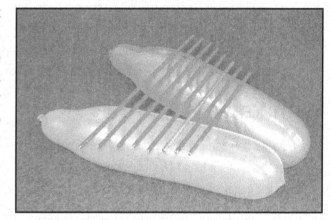

Place the rods across the two balloons resting on the double-sided tape as shown in the picture. With balloon mounting, it's not crucial to have the correct amount of overhang.

PLAYING THE RODS ON BALLOONS

Strike the rods near the centers with the felt tip pens or a small spoon.

ANY POTENTIAL PROBLEMS?

See the Technical Note on the left for a note on fine-tuning the rods.

For more on scales & tunings, see pages 107–110.

FURTHER POSSIBILITIES

With the steel rod instrument, you can create different tunings or add more notes to your scale by cutting more rods to different lengths. See the "Useful Information" sidebar near the start of this chapter for tuning principles.

ACOUSTIC NOTES

The balloons offer two great advantages as a support system. One is that they're so pliable that they scarcely inhibit the vibration at all, allowing the bars to vibrate very freely. As a result, metal bars on balloons ring with a clear tone and long sustain. The other advantage of balloons is that they readily pick up the vibrations from the bars. Then, with their large surface area, the balloons do a great job of projecting the sound out into the air. They especially help with the lower tones, creating a fuller, richer sound. This is good for bars that don't have a lot of surface area of their own, as with the ¼" rods. (They're so narrow they'd be scarcely audible without the help of the balloons).

BAMBOO WOODBLOCKS

These bamboo woodblocks have tone similar to a percussionist's wood blocks and temple blocks — a strong, clear "thok!" sound. A set of several of them with different tones makes an excellent instrument. The following plan is for a randomly tuned set, but they can also be deliberately tuned, as explained under "Further Possibilities" below.

PROCEDURE

For six bamboo woodblocks, cut six segments of bamboo to varied lengths between about 8 and 18 inches long. It is not important if there are joints in the segment or where in the segment they are located.

Using sand paper, round over the newly cut edges so they won't splinter. The easiest way to do this is to lay the sandpaper flat on a table top or other surface, and draw the bamboo edges across it.

For each bamboo segment, cut four snippets of weatherstrip about ¾" long.

On each bamboo segment, at a point between a fourth and a fifth of the length from each end, attach two of the snippets of weatherstripping using the adhesive backing. Place them 90 degrees apart (see the drawings on the facing page). The pads will serve as feet, holding the bamboo up off the surface so it can vibrate freely when struck.

SKILL LEVEL

This instrument requires cutting bamboo with a saw.

MATERIALS

Bamboo, about 10 feet. The diameter should be about an inch and a quarter or larger. Available at nurseries and garden supply centers.

Adhesive-backed foam weather stripping in the thickest available size (7/16" thick by ¾" wide is a standard size that works well.) You won't need more than a couple of feet, so the smallest amount you can purchase will be enough. Get the densest, firmest sort you can find, such as the stuff sold as closed-cell neoprene sponge rubber. Available at hardware stores.

Two hard, medium-heavy beaters. Wooden spoons work well. Metal table spoons are an acceptable second choice.

Optional: A moisture-blocking **wood finish** to reduce potential splitting in the bamboo. This could be almost any commercial wood finish, beeswax, or even white glue. Only a very small amount is needed.

TOOLS

Carpenter's saw or hacksaw to cut the bamboo

Sandpaper.

Scissors to cut the weather strip.

Optional: **bench vise or large C clamp**. It will be easier for children to cut the bamboo with a vise to hold it steady during sawing.

Above: The bamboo rests on the pads of weatherstripping.

Left: End-on view showing the positioning of the pads.

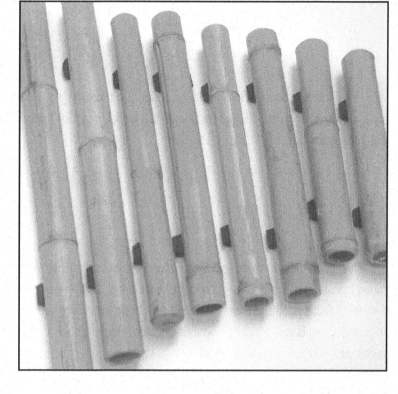

PLAYING THE BAMBOO WOODBLOCKS

Position the six bamboo woodblocks on the floor or a table in any arrangement you like. Strike them near the middle. With wooden spoon beaters, strike with the side of the head of the spoon. With metal table spoons, strike with the round bottom of the head of the spoon.

For more on mallets & beaters: see pages 102–104.

ANY POTENTIAL PROBLEMS?

The weatherstrip may permanently squash if the bamboo segments are stored for a long time with pressure on the pads. Be sure to use the densest, springiest weather stripping you can find, and keep pressure off the pads when storing (leave the bamboos lying on their backs).

FURTHER POSSIBILITIES

Instead of making a randomly tuned set, you can tune the bamboo woodblocks. Because the bamboo is irregularly shaped, the tuning process isn't predictable, but you can tune by following these rules: to raise the pitch of a bamboo segment, shorten it. To lower the pitch, either cut a new piece a little longer, or thin the bamboo at its midpoint by filing or grinding a shallow groove halfway around the underside.

You can make more than the suggested six bamboo segments to have a fuller scale. The instrument heard in the recording, for instance (track 20), is a tuned set of eight bamboos. The bamboos can sound good over a large musical range, so it's possible to make sets much larger still.

If you're really ambitious, consider building a framework and laying out the bamboos like the bars of a marimba. See the sidebar on page 36 for more information.

For more on scales & tunings, see pages 107–110

For an improved version of the instrument, use a higher quality sponge rubber for the pads.* Cut it to a shallow cradle shape to fit the bamboo, and glue it in place.

---

*Suitable high-quality sponge rubber is not commonly available at hardware stores or foam shops. It is available from Experimental Musical Instruments at www.windworld.com.

TUBULAR CHIMES

Metal tubes produce a lovely musical sound. On these pages you'll find a plan for a tubular chime set, followed by several additional ideas for things you can do with metal tubes.

Tubulon (EMT Chimes)

This tuned tubular chime set is a clear and fine-sounding instrument. It can be tuned by cutting to the lengths given in the chart below, and it never needs retuning. Two mounting systems are described below – rope mounting and box mounting. Rope mounting is easier but box mounting is more elegant, holds the tubes in place better, and produces a better sound.

PROCEDURE

Cut the tubes to the lengths given below. The job of cutting is easiest if you use a tubing cutter with the tubes held in a vise. Mark each pipe with its pitch.

Pitch	Length (inches)	Length (cm)
C	14 $7/_{16}$"	36.7cm
D	13 $11/_{16}$"	34.7cm
E	12 $7/_8$"	32.7cm
G	11 $13/_{16}$"	30.0cm
A	11 $1/_8$"	28.3cm
C	10 $3/_{16}$"	25.9cm

Set-up for the rope-mounted version:

Lay the tubes out on the rope as shown in the photo on the facing page. Between a fourth and a fifth of each tube should overhang at each end.

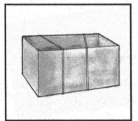

Set-up for the box-mounted version:

Fold the top-flaps of the box down into the box. This will get them out of the way and help reinforce the sides.

Stretch two pairs of 7" rubber bands around the box slightly angled as shown in the drawing.

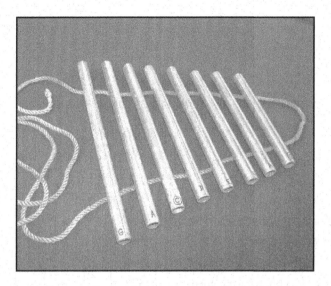

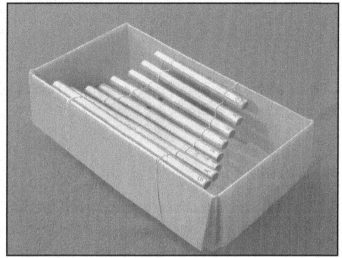

Insert the tubes between the rubber bands in the over-under-over-under pattern shown in the photo below. Arrange it so the rubber bands

hold the tubes at a point between a fourth and fifth of the tube length from each end (you don't have to be precise about this). The rubber bands will stretch and sag under the weight of the tubes; that's ok.

PLAYING THE TUBULON

Strike the tubes near the center. If you're using wooden spoons for the beaters, strike with the side of the spoon head.

ANY POTENTIAL DIFFICULTIES WITH THIS INSTRUMENT?

In the rope-mounted version, the tubes will dance out of position with vigorous playing. When this happens, simply reposition them.

In the box-mounted version, the rubber bands won't last forever. They'll last longer if the instrument is disassembled before long periods of storage.

If you plan to play these tubes with other instrument tuned to standard pitch, see the "Technical Note" sidebar on page 33 for a word on the fine-tuning of the tubes.

FURTHER POSSIBILITIES

If you like this instrument, you might want to make a more permanent framework for it. The "Making Support Frameworks" sidebar on page 38 has a few helpful hints about that.

The tube lengths given on page 36 will give you a C major pentatonic scale over one octave. You can give your instrument a different scale or make more tubes to give it a wider musical range. The "Useful Information" sidebar on page 31 has information on bar and tube tuning. If you wish to extend the range of the instrument much lower, it would be a good idea to use larger diameter tubing (like 1") for the lower notes.

For more on scales & tunings, see pages 107–110.

More Ideas for Tubular Chimes

Here are two more things you can do with steel tubing. (See the previous plan for information on cutting the tubing and suggestions for sizes and tuning.)

HANGING CHIMES

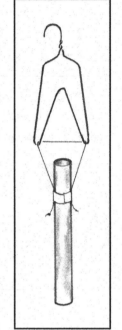

The tubes of the EMT chime set described above can make a nice set of hanging chimes.

To sound their best, chimes are hung from a suspension point located around 22% of the chime length from one end. Children can use adhesive tape to attach a length of cord for suspension at that point. The drawing shows an easy way to bend a coat hanger to provide a hook for the suspension cord. Use the cord-plus-coat hanger to suspend chimes from a tree branch or other suitable overhang.

Play the hanging chimes just as you do the horizontal ones, by striking near the center with a suitable beater.

WATER-DIPPING CHIMES

Tubular metal chimes can make unusual pitch-bending sounds when one end is dipped in water. Larger chimes work better than smaller for this.

From among the chimes in the tubular chime set in the previous plan, choose the largest one. Or, better, start with tubing of larger diameter and make a bigger chime. Use adhesive tape to attach a suspension cord at 22% of the tube length as described above for the hanging chimes. If you don't happen to be near a pond or swimming pool, fill a bucket with water.

Find a suitable beater such as a large wooden spoon. (If the dipping chime is quite large, then something larger and heavier than the wooden spoon might be called for.) While holding the looped cord in one hand, use the other hand to strike the chime at the center with the beater. Slowly dip the chime into the water while striking repeatedly. Experiment to find the best wobbly pitch-bending effects.

MAKING SUPPORT FRAMEWORKS FOR BAR INSTRUMENTS

With a little more work, adults or near-adults can design frameworks for many of the bar instruments in this section. This will make them both more elegant and more permanent.

You can use either of two systems for supporting the sounding bars or tubes: suspending them on cords or resting them on pads. There are many different ways to handle each of these methods. Whatever system you devise, remember to locate the support points between a fourth and a fifth of the length (22%) from the ends of the bars or tubes, and be sure they are not held rigidly.

XYLOPHONE

MATERIALS

1x4 board, 16 feet (two 8-foot boards or three 6-foot boards will do). 1" x 4" is the nominal size; the actual dimensions of the board as purchased from the lumber yard typically are somewhat smaller and that's OK. Look for boards with straight, close grain and without knots. Different species of wood have different sound qualities, but any species will work. It's important that the wood be dry and well seasoned, as unseasoned wood will go out of tune quickly. If you're able to pay more, get KD (kiln-dried) wood.

2x4 board, 6 feet (two 3-foot lengths). Any kind of wood.

Adhesive-backed foam rubber weather stripping, 5/16" thick or more, six feet. Get a dense, firm sort, not soft and squishy.

18 rubber bands. Size 64, which is the common ¼" x 3 ½" size, is suitable.

A pair of medium-soft, medium-heavy beaters. Try large plastic spoons (the sort used as servers for non-stick pans), or large wooden spoons padded with moleskin or other padding material.

TOOLS

Carpentry saw or hacksaw.

File or sandpaper.

For the tuned version only: **an instrument to tune to,** such as an electronic keyboard instrument or a piano.

The prefix *xylo* means wood. The xylophone described here is a wooden bar instrument.

A simple xylophone can be a stand-out instrument in a children's ensemble. It's easy to play, and the tone convincingly cuts through other sounds and sounds great!

PROCEDURE

For a random-pitch instrument

Cut nine bars to a range of lengths between 12" and 21" (the exact lengths aren't important). Use sandpaper or a file to round over the newly cut edges to prevent splintering. Ignore the following several paragraphs about tuning, and skip ahead to the instructions for laying out the bars.

For a tuned instrument

Look at the lengths chart on the following page. Start by cutting the longest, lowest pitch bar (C at 21½").

Because wood is unpredictable, this piece probably won't give the intended pitch at first. It still needs to be fine-tuned. Tuning is done by comparing the bar's note to the

For more on scales & tunings, see pages 107–110.

For more on mallets & beaters: see pages 102–104.

intended note on an electronic keyboard instrument, piano, or other instrument. To sound the bar, hold it loosely as shown in the picture and strike it at the middle with a wooden spoon or other suitable beater.

If the bar's pitch is lower than the C on the keyboard, make the pitch higher by cutting it a bit shorter. Try cutting off a half inch if it's far too low; less if it seems pretty close. Check the pitch again. Still to low? Cut a little shorter.

If the bar's tone is too high, use the saw to make a shallow cut across what is to be the underside of the bar at the middle as shown in the picture. Don't make this cut too deep – try about an eighth of an inch if the bar was far too high; less if it was pretty close. Check the pitch again. Still to high? Make the cut a little deeper.

When you've got a good pitch-match, use a file or sand paper to round off the newly cut edges slightly to prevent splintering.

Proceed through all nine bars in this fashion, cutting to the recommended length and tuning by comparison to the intended pitch on the keyboard.

Lengths Chart, very approximate

C	21½"	55.5cm
D	20¼"	51.5cm
E	19"	48.5cm
G	17½"	44.5cm
A	16½"	42cm
c	15¼"	38.5cm
d	14½"	36.5cm
e	13½"	34.5cm
g	12½"	32cm

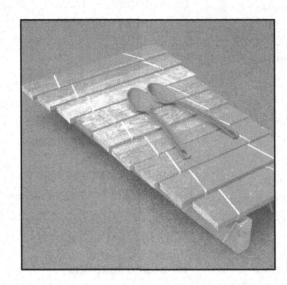

Laying Out the Bars

Cut two 2x4s to 36" long.

Cut two 36" segments of weatherstripping. Use the adhesive backing to attach a strip to one edge of each 2x4.

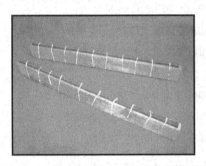

Place nine rubber bands around each 2x4 and space the rubber bands apart approximately evenly.

Lay the bars out on the 2x4s as shown in the photo, with the 2x4s slightly out of parallel. Slip the ends of the bars through the rubber bands to keep the bars in place. The ideal is to have between a fourth and a fifth of each bar overhanging the mounting pads at each end. You won't be able to get this perfectly for most of the bars, but by spacing the 2x4s about the right distance apart you can come reasonably close.

PLAYING THE XYLOPHONE

Strike the bars near their centers with the mallets (large plastic spoons, wooden spoons with padding, or whatever other mallet option you choose).

ANY POTENTIAL DIFFICULTIES?

Tuning the bars is challenging, and may be difficult even for grown-ups.

If you use unseasoned wood to make the bars, they will go out of tune quickly. You can retune if necessary.

If you use very well seasoned or kiln dried wood, the bars will hold the tuning better. You can improve the stability by sealing the ends of the bars with a commercial wood finish, beeswax, or other moisture resistant finish.

FURTHER POSSIBILITIES

You can give this instrument a different scale or increase its range by tuning the bars to different notes or adding more bars.

The set-up suggested here, with the bars resting on 2x4s sitting on the floor or on a table top, has the advantage that it can easily be disassembled for transportation or storage. But you could make a more elegant and permanent instrument by building a frame to support the bars. See the sidebar on page 38 for more information.

ACOUSTIC NOTES

The tuning process for these wooden bars illustrates nicely the two tuning principles for bar percussion outlined in the sidebar on page 31. Shortening the bar reduces the amount of weight in the parts of the bar that move the most, making the pitch higher. Making the shallow saw cut across the middle makes it less rigid at the center flex-point, making the pitch lower.

BUCKET DRUMS

SKILL LEVEL

The main requirement for constructing this instrument is cutting heavy cord with scissors. For playing, the child should be big enough to wear the bucket using a shoulder strap.

MATERIALS

Two or three plastic buckets. Audition as many different buckets as you can get your hands on and select the two or three best sounding among them to be your keepers. Some possibilities are five-gallon buckets that various commercial products are sold in, one- or two-gallon versions of the same, plastic potting containers used by nurseries for plants awaiting sale, and plastic household buckets of the sort you'd use for floor-mopping. Smaller buckets are suitable for smaller children. Be sure the buckets are clean and free of residue.

15 feet of cord or strapping material. Any sort of cord, preferably ³/₁₆" to ¼" thick, will do.

Duct tape.

Two heavy, medium-soft beaters. Superball beaters are best. Otherwise try a pair of wooden spoons, preferably overwrapped with a few layers of mole skin, duct tape or rubber bands to make them softer.

For more on mallets & beaters: see pages 104-106.

TOOLS

Scissors to cut the cords and duct tape.

As many street musicians can attest, plastic buckets make excellent drums. To play a plastic bucket, turn it upside down and strike the bottom with beaters. The five-gallon buckets that industrial products come in usually sound good. Other sizes of commercial product containers work well too, as well as plastic household buckets. Two or three buckets with contrasting tones sound especialy good playing together. In this plan, the buckets have shoulder straps, so children can march around while playing them. This way of holding them has another advantage: the buckets sound better when held up off the ground.

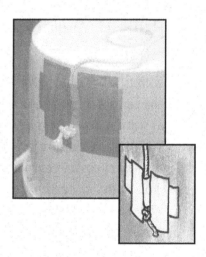

PROCEDURE

Cut a five-foot length of cord for each bucket. Tie a knot at each end of the cord.

Using duct tape, tape the ends of a cord to the sides of one of the buckets as shown in the detail drawing and photo on the right. Use fairly long strips of tape to give it plenty of holding power, and be sure to press it down well so it really sticks. Now try the bucket-and-strap on for size. Place the strap over one shoulder so the bucket hangs down the opposite side. The ideal hanging height is low on the hip, well below the waist. If the strap length needs adjusting to get this height, remove the tape at one end of the cord, re-tape it to lengthen or shorten the strap as needed, and try it on again.

When you've got the strap right, repeat the procedure for the other bucket(s).

PLAYING THE BUCKET DRUMS

A small child can wear one bucket over the shoulders. Bigger kids can wear two buckets at once, assuming the buckets aren't too huge, and some may be able to manage three. Alternatively, put three buckets on three kids. Play them by striking with mallets. Hit in different parts of the top to get different tones. For variety, get additional sounds by striking the sides of the buckets, and by hitting with the hard part of the mallet handle.

If the bucket handle rattles, tape firmly over the handle connection to immobilize it.

FURTHER POSSIBILITIES

You can have still more fun if you go beyond two or three buckets, building up a battery of drums with several buckets and perhaps a few metallic pots and other bangable things as well. But how to hold these objects? Many of them don't sound well when they're just resting on the ground. Here are a couple of possibilities (probably more suitable as building projects for adults than for children). Option 1: design a framework to hold the buckets up and away from the floor, with the opening mostly unobstructed. Option 2: cut a hole in the side of each plastic bucket so that the air inside isn't trapped even when the bucket rests on the ground. The hole should be fairly large, like six inches or so diameter in a large bucket, located closer to the rim than the playing surface (thanks to Jody Kruskal for this idea). With both of these projects, it's good to have the buckets rest on pads rather than hard surfaces, to avoid rattles and thuds.

Another possibility is to use large, hard plastic water bottles rather than or in addition to buckets. The water bottles come in two large sizes: 3-gallon and 5-gallon. The playing technique is as simple as can be imagined: sit on the edge of an armless chair, turn the bottle upside down, hold it between your knees, and play its bottom like a conga drum. They sound excellent played by hand, but for children it's preferable, for hand protection, to use medium-soft mallets such as superball mallets. The sound from these instruments is fairly loud, more "rounded," and a bit longer lasting than is usual for drums. The contrast between the tone of the 5-gallon variety and its higher-sounding 3-gallon cousin makes for attractive duet possibilities. One often finds old bottles that have been discarded because they've cracked. The cracks, usually on the sides or near the neck, don't noticeably harm the tone. These drums/bottles are suitable for any child big enough to hold them between the knees.

ACOUSTIC NOTES

The sound from the bucket drum comes from both the playing surface and the air inside. If you block off the open end by setting the drum flat on the ground, the enclosed air is blocked off and deadened, and a part of the sound is lost. With the plastic bottle drums just mentioned above, the large resonating air space inside and the relatively narrow opening make a particularly rich and long-sustaining tone.

SKILL LEVEL

The components are assembled in a way that requires some manual dexterity. Recommended for ages 8 and up.

MATERIALS

8-ounce plastic yogurt container or similar plastic container.

CD or DVD (choose one you no longer need).

Several large, flat rubber bands, size 64 (that's the common 3½" x ¼" size).

String, about 5 feet.

TOOLS

None.

If a strong current of wind passes over a string, it can set the string vibrating. With a string stretched across a small, light framework, you can sound the string by whirling the framework through the air on the end of a cord. Flat rubber bands are the perfect stringing material for this because ribbon-shaped strings are especially responsive to air currents. The tone of a rubber-band whirler is like the buzzing of an insect, with the sound rising and falling as the whirler whirls.

The frame for such an instrument can take many forms. The plan on this page uses a plastic yogurt container and a CD, held together with some rubber bands that also serve as the strings. The rubber-band strings can be tuned, though not with precision. With an ensemble of children playing whirled strings tuned to different pitches, you can create musical pieces by having the children play in sequence or play together in a buzzing sort of harmony.

For information on the group playing technique called "hocketing," see page 113.

PROCEDURE

Place the rubber bands on the CD/yogurt assembly as shown in the photo below. You can go with two, three or four rubber bands. The vibrating segments of each rubber band (the segments spanning from the edge of the CD to the rim of the yogurt container) should be free of any twists.

Tie one end of the string to the rubber bands where they intersect in the middle of the bottom of the container.

Tuning the instrument is optional. To tune, vary the amount of stretch on the vibrating segments of the rubber bands by pulling the rubber band around and over the CD or the bottom of the container. Check the pitch by plucking the rubber band segments. If you want your whirled strings to produce one note, tune all the segments to the same note. For a two-note whirler, tune half of the segments to one note and half to another.

PLAYING THE WHIRLED STRINGS

Whirl the yogurt/CD assembly on the string until it starts to sing. This is best as an outdoor instrument; play in a large space with other people at a safe distance.

ANY POTENTIAL DIFFICULTIES?

The yogurt containers are good for kid-whirling because they're light and less dangerous than a heavier framework

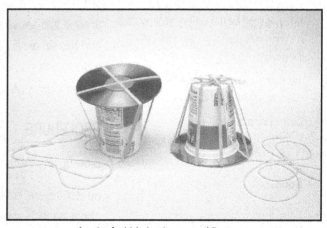

A pair of whirled string assemblies

would be. But by the same token they're a little weak and they may deform under the stress of the rubber bands.

FURTHER POSSIBILITIES

A sturdier framework, in addition to being more durable (and more dangerous), may also sound better. Any design of suitable size and weight will do as long as it supports the rubber bands with their vibrating segments out and away from the framework in a way that allows them to catch the wind.

The most impressive whirled strings use very large rubber bands (such as the size labeled as size #107, available at office supply outlets such as Office Depot or www.quill.com).

A very successful type of large whirlers called spirit catchers was created by the late catcher of spirits, Darrell DeVore. These have very large rubber bands forming a diamond around a cross-shaped framework of wooden dowels.

ACOUSTIC NOTES

When the whirled strings whirl, the air rushing past the strings sets up patterns of turbulence, and this gives rise to the sound. Having a sound board is less important for an air-driven instrument such as this because the vibration arises in the air itself, making the soundboard's role of transmitting to the air less crucial.

BALLOONCHORDS

CD TRACK 25

Here are two plans for making rubber band string instruments with balloons.

SKILL LEVEL

Balloonbody Balloonchord: The hardest part is blowing up and tying the balloons. If an adult handles that, then this instrument is simple enough for small children.

Balloonchord zither: one saw cut is required in addition to blowing and tying the balloon.

MATERIALS

Two sausage-shaped balloons.

Several rubber bands. The widely available 1/16" x 3" size (referred to as #18), is good for this project. Wide, flat rubber bands don't work as well for this instrument.

Two unsharpened pencils, chopsticks or similar-sized sticks.

Cellophane tape.

TOOLS

None.

BALLOONBODY BALLOONCHORD

The balloonbody balloonchord consists of several rubber bands stretched around two sausage-shaped balloons. The balloons project the sound quite well, and this simple arrangement makes a clear and pleasing string sound. If you're not a perfectionist about it, you can tune the rubber bands to a recognizable scale … or don't worry about tuning and enjoy a random tuning.

PROCEDURE

Blow up and tie the balloons.

Stretch several rubber bands around the two balloons as shown in the photo, spaced about an inch apart. Locate them more toward one end of the balloons, leaving

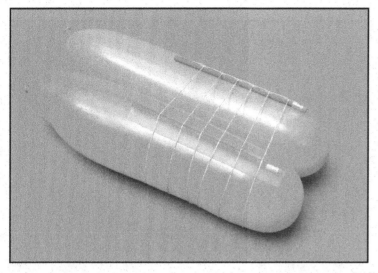

rubber band. For this reason the tape isn't centered on the pencil, but overhangs on the non-playing side.

Do the same with another piece of tape for the other pencil or chopstick.

PLAYING THE BALLOONBODY BALLOONCHORD

Pluck the rubber band segments that stretch between the pencils or chopsticks. If you pluck very hard, the rubber band will snap against the balloons and make a sharp snapping sound. This is good for an occasional effect, but the tone of softer plucking is nicer. (For a fun variation on the snap sound, see the "Further Possibilities" on page 46.) Optional: by playing in a sitting position, you can cross your legs in a way that holds the end of the balloons where there aren't any rubber bands. This allows you to pluck with both hands.

When the rubber bands are first put on, the tuning is random. You can control the tuning by pulling and sliding the rubber bands one way or the other so that the segment between the balloons becomes tighter (for higher notes) or looser (for lower). To do this, carefully slide the rubber band in one direction or the other under the tape.

about eight inches at the other end without rubber bands.

Slip two unsharpened pencils or chopsticks under the rubber bands as shown in the photo.

Cellophane tape is needed to keep the rubber band strings in position while playing. Pull off a piece of tape a little shorter than the pencils or chopsticks. Place the tape over the rubber bands along one of the pencils or chopsticks as shown in the drawing. Important: the tape shouldn't interfere with the vibrating part of the

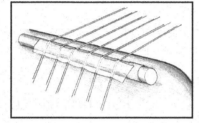

BALLOONCHORD ZITHER

This instrument is a little louder than the balloonbody balloonchord described above, and produces lower notes. It can be tuned more accurately, and the tone has a dark and deep quality.

PROCEDURE

Cut the 1x4 or 2x4 board to two feet long. (If the cut is not very accurate, that's OK.)

Blow up and tie the balloon.

Place a seven-inch rubber band around the board longways, then slip the balloon underneath. Instead of centering it, position the balloon closer to one end of the board as shown in the photo.

With the rubber band holding the balloon in place, add three more seven-inch rubber bands parallel to the first one, so that you end up with four rubber bands spaced about an inch apart.

Insert the two pencils to form bridges under the rubber bands as shown in the drawing.

To keep the rubber bands in place, put tape across the bridges in the manner described for the balloonbody balloonchord on page 43, being sure that the tape doesn't interfere with the active part of the string.

PLAYING THE BALLOONCHORD ZITHER

Pluck the rubber-band strings on either side of the balloon.

You can leave the tuning random, or adjust the tuning to your liking. To tune, pull and slide the rubber bands around the edge where they cross the board so that the playing segment becomes tighter (for higher notes) or looser (for lower). The shorter segments on one side of the balloon typically make higher notes than the longer segments on the other side.

FURTHER POSSIBILITIES

There's an alternative version for both balloon chord instruments that is a little easier to make. If you simply omit the pencil-bridges and place the tape directly to the balloon surface, then the rubber-band-strings snap against the bal-

loons each time you pluck, creating a louder sound with a slightly wacky effect.

With either of the balloonchords you can add more notes by adding more rubber bands.

ANY POTENTIAL DIFFICULTIES?

The balloons and rubber bands won't last forever, but they're usually good for a several days.

A very small percentage of people are allergic to the latex used in making rubber bands and balloons.

ACOUSTIC NOTES

For musical strings to do a good job of projecting their sound into the air, they need something that can act as a soundboard, as discussed in the acoustic notes for box zithers on page 12. It happens that balloons make excellent soundboards for lightweight, low-tension strings like rubber bands.

The wonderful term "plosive aerophones" refers to instruments in which the air inside a tube or other enclosure is excited by some kind of percussive blow. For example, imagine that you take a tube and slap one end with the sole of a beach sandal. The slap gives a jolt to the air in the tube, causing a brief but clear tone at the tube's natural frequency. That's a plosive aerophone sound. A set of such tubes, tuned by cutting to different lengths, makes a fine musical instrument. This is one of many forms that plosive aerophones can take. On the following pages there are several more.

Plosive aerophones make good home-made instrument projects because they're easy to make and easy to play, and they sound great. Also, they're predictably tunable: the tube lengths can be specified in a plan, and a well tuned scale will result without needing any further tuning.*

SKILL LEVEL

The maker of this instrument will have to do some measurements and handle sharp scissors.

MATERIALS

Golf club tubes, available at sporting goods stores. To make the basic six-note version of the instrument you'll need to purchase six golf tubes. For the full fifteen-note version you need to purchase nine.

TOOLS

Scissors.

Measuring tape or yard stick.

GOLF CLUB TUBES

This plan is for a set of side-struck tubes. The tone comes when you hit the side of the tube, giving the air inside a jolt. This works well only if the tube wall is soft enough to flex when struck. But where to get tubing that has just the right degree of softness? One answer is golf club tubes.** These are lightweight plastic tubes, 1¼" in diameter and 34" long, used by golfers to protect their clubs when they're loaded into a golf bag. They're available for about a dollar apiece at sporting goods stores. They can be cut to length with nothing more than good scissors.

The first version of this plan is for a set of tuned golf tubes to be played handheld in pairs. Each player holds a tube in each hand and slaps them against his or her knees or calves, a wall, the floor, a table edge … almost anything solid, but preferably not a passing stranger. Several players working together can play rhythms and melodies using all the tubes.

The second version of the plan is for the same set of tubes, but mounted in a way that allows one player to play all the tubes with mallets or beaters.

With either version you have a choice of how many tubes you want to make, from six for a basic version to fifteen for the deluxe model.

---

*Experimental Musical Instruments has put out a book and CD called *Slap tubes and Other Plosive Aerophones* devoted to the making of these instruments, available from www.windworld.com.

**Thanks to Phil Dadson for suggesting this widely available and perfectly suited tubing.

Golf Tubes Version 1: Hand-held

PROCEDURE

Cut the tubes to the lengths indicated in the chart below. (The instructions there will help you decide if you want your version of the instrument to have six notes, eight notes, or more.) A note concerning precision: the lengths in the chart are accurate to 1/16", but if younger children have a hard time with this degree of precision, don't worry. Anything within about a quarter inch will yield recognizable scales.

Some golf tubes come with a hidden reinforcing wire circling one end. This wire tends to rattle. In shortening the tube, cut off that end.

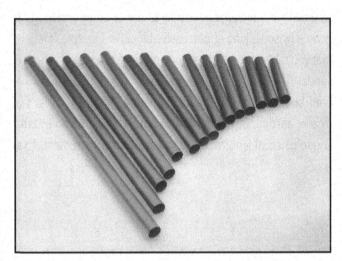

Golf Tube Lengths

Note	Length (inches)	Length (cm)
G3	33¾"	85.7cm
A3	30"	76.2cm
B3	26⅝"	67.6cm
C4	25⅛"	63.8cm
D4	22⁵⁄₁₆"	56.7cm
E4	19¾"	50.2cm
F4	18⅝"	47.3cm
G4	16½"	41.9cm
A4	14⅝"	37.1cm
B5	12¹⁵⁄₁₆"	32.7cm
C5	12¹⁄₁₆"	30.6cm
D5	10¾"	27.3cm
E5	9½"	24.1cm
F5	8¹⁵⁄₁₆"	22.7cm
G5	7⅞"	20.0cm

This chart gives lengths for a total of 15 notes forming a diatonic scale (seven notes per octave) over two octaves with C as the home tone.

You don't have to make all 15 tubes. Choose one of these options:

6 tubes – 1-octave five-note scale (pentatonic). Cut to the lengths in bold print above the dividing line in the chart.

8 tubes – 1-octave seven-note scale (diatonic). Cut to all the lengths above the dividing line.

11 tubes – 2-octave pentatonic. Cut to all the lengths in bold.

15 tubes – 2 octaves diatonic. Cut to all the lengths in the chart.

PLAYING THE GOLF TUBES

Hold a tube in each hand, and slap the sides of the tubes against any suitable solid object, wall or floor. To play different notes, pick up and put down different tubes as needed. Alternatively, form a small ensemble with several people playing two tubes each.

For more on scales & tunings, see pages 107–110.

For information on the group playing technique called "hocketing," see page 113.

Even though the notes of this scale run from G to G, the notes are those of a C scale, with C as the tonal center.

Golf Tubes Version 2: Mounted

MATERIALS

The tuned golf tube set described in the previous plan.

Yardstick or other similar stick.

Rubber bands. Size #64 (¼" x 3 ½") is good.

Towel or pillow.

Two small spoons for beaters.

TOOLS

Same as in the previous plan.

PLAYING THE INSTRUMENT

Strike the tubes with the spoons near where they cross the cross piece.

PROCEDURE

Cut a set of tuned golf tubes as described in the previous plan.

The yardstick will serve as a cross-support piece for the tuned tubes. To attach the tuned tubes to the yardstick, use rubber bands. Follow the steps shown in the drawings below.

Do this for all the tubes.

Lay the assembly of tubes on the folded towel.

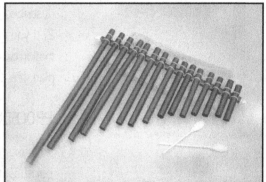

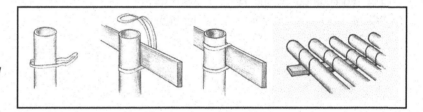

CORRUGATED PLASTIC FLEX TUBES

This is a variation on the golf tubes plan above, but using corrugated plastic flex tubing in place of the golf tubes. (It's the same sort of tubing used in the plan for whirlies on page 15.) As side-struck tubes the corrugated plastic doesn't sound quite as nice as the golf tubes, but it has some unique qualities, namely ...

1) For a really unusual tone quality, corrugated tubes can be played by scraping as described under "Playing the Instrument" below.

2) If you play by swinging a corrugated tube against a hard surface, then the swinging motion excites a ghostly trace of the whirly tone described in the Whirled Corrugaphones plan. It's a subtle but enchanting effect, coming just before the strike.

PROCEDURE

To make the corrugated tube set, follow the procedures of the golf tube plan above, but substitute the lengths given below. If you also make the instrument called Whirled Corrugaphones (see the plan on page 15), you can use some of the corrugated tubes for both instruments.

G	62"	157cm
A	57"	145cm
B	50"	127cm
C	47"	119cm
D	42½"	108cm
E	37½"	95cm
F	35"	89cm
G	31½"	80cm
A	28"	20cm
B	25"	63.5cm
C	23½"	59.5cm
D	20 ½"	52cm
E	18"	45.5cm
F	17"	43cm
G	15¼"	38.5cm
A	13½"	34.5cm
B	12"	30.5cm
C	11¼"	28.5cm

This chart gives lengths for a total of 18 notes, forming a complete diatonic scale over two and a half octaves with C as the home tone.

You don't have to make all 18. Choose one of these options.

6 tubes – 1-octave five-note scale (pentatonic). Cut to the lengths in bold print between the two dividing lines in the chart.

8 tubes – 1-octave seven-note scale (diatonic). Cut to all the lengths between the dividing lines.

13 tubes – 2½-octave five note scale (pentatonic). Cut to all the lengths in bold

18 tubes – 2½-octave seven-note scale (diatonic). Cut to all the lengths in the chart.

PLAYING THE INSTRUMENT

You can play these tubes just as described for the golf tube set above, either hand-held or mounted on a cross-piece and struck with beaters.

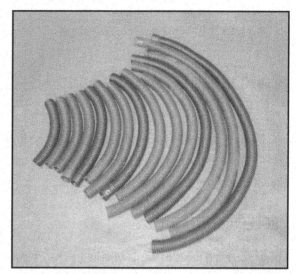

In addition, you can try some scraping sounds:

If yours is a hand-held tube set, scrape any two of the corrugated tubes together. Different pairings create different harmonies and, as you can hear on the CD track 27, it's a wonderfully peculiar sound.

If you made the version with the tubes rubber-banded to a cross bar, sound them by scraping the sides of the tubes with the handle of a spoon. To do this, hold the cross bar in the air so that the tubes hang down free. (For scraping, they sound better this way than they do resting on a pad.) Hold with one hand and scrape with the other.

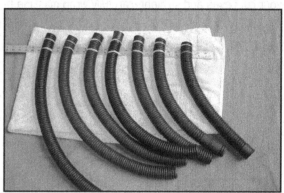

MAILING TUBE SLAP TUBE SET

Back on page 47 I talked about getting a tone from a tube by hitting the open end with a beach sandal. This plan is for a five-note version of that project.

PROCEDURE

Cut six sounding tubes to the lengths in the chart below. To help make your cuts even and straight, carefully wrap masking tape around the tube circumference at the cut-off location and use the tape as a cutting guide. Leave one of the factory-cut ends as one end of each tube.

Note	Length (inches)	Length (cm)
C4	24"	61cm
D4	21³⁄₈"	54.3cm
E4	18⁷⁄₈"	47.9cm
G4	15⁵⁄₈"	39.7cm
A4	13¾"	34.9cm
C5	11¹⁄₈"	28.3cm

The lengths in this chart are accurate to 1/8 of an inch, but children don't need to be that precise. The scale will still be recognizable as long as the cuts are within about a quarter of an inch.

MATERIALS

Seven 24" mailing tubes, 2" diameter. The type with flat-cut ends, not the crimped-end style, is preferable but not required (see the picture below).

Fourteen #64 rubber bands. (This is the common 3½"x ¼" size.)

One sandal from a pair of foam rubber beach sandals (sometimes called zoris, flip flops, thongs, or jandals). If you don't have any around, they are available inexpensively at variety stores. If you can't locate the foam rubber ones, other sandals of similar weight and hardness will do. Avoid ones that have deep patterns cut into the sole.

TOOLS

Hacksaw

Yard stick or tape measure

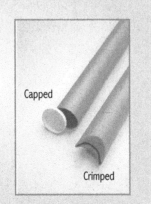

MAILING TUBES Two Types

There are two types of mailing tubes. One comes with a plastic end-cap, while the other has a crimped end that folds in to close the tube. For some of the instruments in this book that use mailing tubes, it doesn't matter which type you use. For others, one type or the other is preferable. If that's the case, the plan's materials list will tell you which type to use.

Capped

Crimped

The materials list called for seven tubes, six for playing and one more to serve as a support piece. The support piece doesn't need to be cut. To prevent it from acting as a sounding tube itself, stuff the ends with tissue paper.

Place two rubber bands loosely around the longest sounding tube (the C tube) near the factory-cut end. Use the rubber bands to attach it near one end of the support tube as shown in the drawing on the facing page. Do the same for the other five sounding tubes, positioning them as shown in the photo and drawing.

PLAYING THE SLAP TUBES

Hold the support tube with one hand near the end where there's room to hold. With the other hand, strike the open ends of the sounding tubes with the beach sandal. The sole of the sandal should come down as flat as possible over the tube ends. The sound is best when the sandal completely covers the tube end and then instantaneously bounces off.

ANY POTENTIAL PROBLEMS?

The highest notes on this instrument may sometimes come out a little flat of the intended pitch. This happens when the beach sandal covers the tube end for too long instead of bouncing right off. You can learn to hit in a way that avoids this problem.

Cardboard mailing tubes are softer than would be ideal for these instruments, but they work reasonably well and they are more kid-friendly than the alternatives.

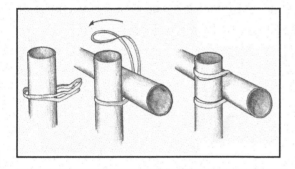

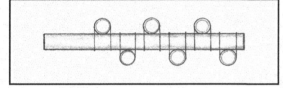

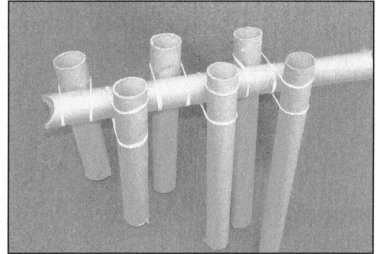

LARGE STAMPING TUBES AND END-STRUCK CAPPED TUBES

Stamping tubes are tubes closed at one end, sounded by thumping the closed end on a solid surface such as pavement or hard ground. The tubes can be large or small. The large ones make a particularly impressive bass tone. Traditional bamboo stamping tubes have been played in many parts of the world, sometimes in groups of marching street musicians.

For another playing technique and sound, the stamping tubes described here can also be used as end-struck tubes. Instructions for reconfiguring the tubes for that purpose can be found following the stamping tube plans below. The end-struck tone is sharper and edgier than the stamping tube tone.

In place of bamboo (hard to get in such large sizes), the plans below plans offer a choice of materials. First is a version made from 3" cardboard mailing tubes. Second is one using PVC plastic tubing. PVC is less expensive, longer lasting, better-sounding, more accurately tunable, and suitable for making an instrument with a wider range of notes. But many people see it as environmentally objectionable, and some will prefer not to use it with children. If you do work with it, a breathing mask and goggles will be needed for the cutting.

Cardboard Stamping Tubes

SKILL LEVEL

The cardboard mailing tubes are to be measured and cut with a hacksaw.

PROCEDURE

Cut the sounding-tubes to the lengths given on the chart below. Optional: To help make your cuts even and straight, wrap a layer of masking tape around the tube circumference at the cut-off location and use the tape as a cutting guide.

Note	Length (inches)	Length (cm)
G	34¾ "	88.3cm
A	31"	78.8cm
B	27 ⅝"	70.1cm
C	26 ⅜"	66.9cm
D	23¼"	59cm
E	20 ⅜"	51.8cm
F	19 ⅜"	49.2cm
G	16 ⅝"	42.2mm

This chart gives lengths for a total of eight notes, forming a diatonic scale over one octave with C as the home tone.

You don't have to make all 8. Choose one of these options.

6 tubes – 1-octave five-note scale (pentatonic). Cut to the lengths in bold print.

8 tubes – 1-octave seven-note scale (diatonic). Cut to all the lengths.

Although the scales shown here run from G to G, the notes are those of a C scale.

Place a plastic end stopper in one end of each tube.

MATERIALS

Seven 3" x 36" cardboard mailing tubes with plastic end cover (see the picture on page 52).

TOOLS

Hacksaw or carpenter's saw.

Measuring stick or tape.

Felt-tip marker.

PLAYING THE STAMPING TUBES

For information on the group playing technique called "hocketing," see page 113.

Thump the tubes firmly, closed-end-down, on the floor, pavement, cement block or large stone. Some surfaces sound better than others; for instance, thumping directly on a wooden floor may produce more noise than tone.

Adults can play two tubes, one in each hand. Children will do better with just one. An ensemble of several players can play hocketing style.

ANY POTENTIAL DIFFICULTIES?

The plastic stoppers that come with some brands of mailing tubes are lighter and flimsier than others. This can throw off the tuning. If you need to tune accurately to a standard scale and you find your pitches coming out a bit low, that's probably why. You can correct the tuning by shortening the tube a small amount.

SKILL LEVEL

The cardboard mailing tubes are to be measured and cut with a hack saw.

MATERIALS

In addition to the **materials listed for the previous** plan you'll need:

Several rubber bands, size #64 ($^1/_4$" x 3 $^1/_4$").

Two medium-hard, medium-heavy beaters, such as a pair of wooden spoons.

For more on mallets & beaters: see pages 104—106.

TOOLS

Carpenter's saw or hacksaw.

Measuring stick or tape.

Felt-tip marker.

Cardboard End-Struck Capped Tubes

(Converting the Cardboard Stamping Tubes to End-Struck Tubes)

PROCEDURE

Make the tubes for the stamping tube set as described above.

Use several rubber bands to bundle the tubes together with the capped ends of the tubes together at one end of the bundle. It doesn't matter which tubes end up next to which.

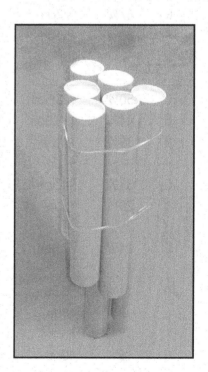

PLAYING THE INSTRUMENT

Alternative playing positions: 1) Sitting perched near the front of a chair, hold the tubes between your legs. 2) Sitting in the chair, rest the tubes across your lap. 3) Rest the tubes on a carpeted floor. Whatever position, make sure the open ends are not blocked.

Strike the capped tube ends with wooden spoons, striking with the side of the head of the spoon. Try striking either on the rim or in the middle of the plastic top.

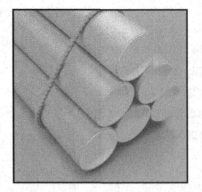

PVC Stamping Tubes

These plastic stamping tubes are much like the cardboard ones described above, but with the plastic you can use longer tubes for a greater range of pitches.

PROCEDURE

Cut the tubes to the lengths given on the chart below. (The notes alongside the chart will help you decide whether to make a complete set of 15 tubes or a smaller set.) To help make your cuts even and straight, wrap a layer of masking tape around the tube circumference at the cut-off location and use the tape as a cutting guide. Cutting will be easier with one person holding the tube and another doing the cutting. Wear a breathing mask and goggles while cutting.

Note	Length (inches)	Length (cm)
G	67¾"	172cm
A	60¼"	153cm
B	53½"	136cm
C	50½"	128.5cm
D	44¾"	113.5cm
E	39¾"	101cm
F	37½"	95cm
G	33¼"	84.5cm
A	29½"	75cm
B	26⅛"	66.5cm
C	24⅝"	62.5cm
D	21¾"	55.5cm
E	19¼"	49cm
F	18⅛"	46cm
G	16"	40cm

This chart gives lengths for a total of fifteen notes, forming a complete diatonic scale over two octaves with C as the home tone.

You don't have to make all 15. Choose one of these options.

6 tubes – 1-octave five-note scale (pentatonic). Cut to the lengths in bold print between the two dividing lines in the chart.

8 tubes – 1-octave seven-note scale (diatonic). Cut to all the lengths between the dividing lines.

11 tubes – 2-octave five note scale (pentatonic). Cut to all the lengths in bold.

15 tubes – 2 octaves seven-note scale (diatonic). Cut to all the lengths in the chart.

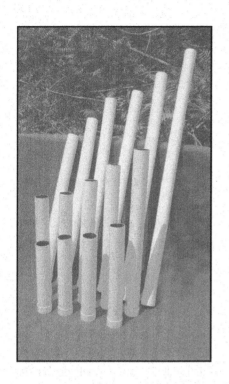

Place an end cap on one end of each tube. Tap it in place by thumping it on the ground, which will also give you a preview of the sound of the tube.

Mark the pitch on each tube.

PLAYING THE INSTRUMENT

Thump the tubes firmly, closed-end-down, on pavement, cement block or large stone. Adults can play two tubes, one in each hand. Children can play one at time, holding it in both hands. An ensemble of several players can play all the tubes at once.

ANY POTENTIAL DIFFICULTIES?

Once again, PVC plastic is envrionmentally objectionable in several respects, and cutting it raises dust.

PVC End-Struck Capped Tubes

(Converting the Stamping Tubes to End-Struck Tubes)

PROCEDURE

Make the tubes for the stamping tube set as described above.

Bundle the tubes together with the two bungee chords, with the capped ends of the tubes together at one end of the bundle. It doesn't matter which tubes end up next to which.

For more on mallets & beaters: see pages 104—106.

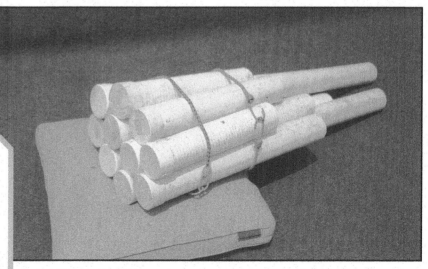

Place the bundle on a large pillow near the capped end. Make sure nothing blocks the open tube ends.

If you'll be using screwdriver handles as beaters, you'll do so by holding by the blade and striking with the handle part. For hand protection, wrap the end of the blade with masking tape, cloth tape or electricians tape before using.

PLAYING THE INSTRUMENT

Strike the capped tube ends with heavy, medium-hard beaters.

FURTHER POSSIBILITIES FOR PLOSIVES

Once you understand how these plosive aerophones work and how effective they are musically, you'll be tempted to make more permanent or more elaborate versions than those described here. You may find yourself thinking about constructing frameworks to hold more tubes. When it comes to a framework design, keep the following considerations in mind:

Think ergonomically. Try to position the tubes for comfortable and convenient playing.

The open ends of tubes should not be obstructed.

Try to have some padding in the mounting of the tubes. If

they are too rigidly held, they transmit the force of each blow through the framework and into the floor, creating thumping and rattling sounds.

ACOUSTIC NOTES

Plosive aerophones make use of the same sort of air vibrations that wind instruments like flutes and clarinets do, but the vibrations are excited in a very different way. In those wind instruments, there's a constant input of energy from the player's blowing, allowing the note to sustain. In the plosives there's no continuous input, just a single stroke causing a sudden percussive sound that dies away quickly.

These instruments are great for crazy groaning and squawking sounds. You can play them in rhythm, too.

Friction drums usually take the form of a drum with a stick or string attached to the middle of the drumhead. The player rubs the stick or string, and the friction is transmitted through the stick or string to vibrate the drumhead.

On these pages are two friction drum designs: one for a string friction drum, and one for a stick friction drum. The drum bodies are empty plastic food containers such as yogurt tubs, with the bottom serving as the drum membrane.

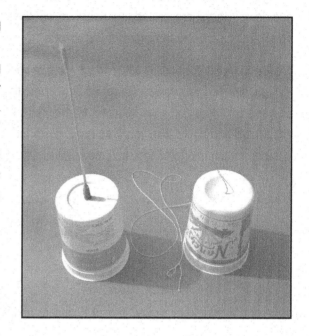

SKILL LEVEL

The maker ties a multiple knot in a string and uses a screwdriver. Suitable for ages 9 and up.

MATERIALS

Large plastic yogurt container or similar container (the 32-ounce size is good).

String, 2 feet.

TOOLS

Scissors (to cut the string).

Thumbtack.

Screwdriver.

Medium-sized screw.

STRING FRICTION DRUM

This string friction drum is good for chicken squawks and mouse squeaks.

PROCEDURE

Start with a clean, empty plastic container with the lid removed. Using a thumbtack, poke a small hole at the center of the bottom of the container. (If the bottom has a little button of thicker plastic at the center, poke just to the side of it.) Using a screwdriver, screw a medium-sized screw into the hole. Then screw it back out, leaving an enlarged hole.

Cut two feet of string. Tie a big knot near one end. To make the knot big, first tie a simple knot. Then overlay another knot in the same place, and another and another, until you have a knot big enough that it won't slip though the hole you just poked.

Slip the un-knotted end of the string through the hole in the bottom of the container from the inside, and pull the string through so that the knot pulls up against the inside bottom of the container.

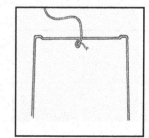

PLAYING THE INSTRUMENT

If you have violin rosin around, rub it all up and down the string to provide better friction. Otherwise, rub the string up and down with the eraser end of a pencil, or wet the string. This increases friction and improves the sound.

The best playing position is seated. Place the container, bottom up, between your knees. Grasp the string near the free end and hold it up and away so that it is straight (but don't pull it hard and tight). With your free hand, pinch the string between thumb and forefinger, and move your hand up and down the string. Try different speeds and pinching pressures to see what gives the best sound.

You can also play standing. Hold the container in one hand. With the other hand, grasp the string between thumb and forefinger close to the container. Sound it by pinching and pulling away from the container, letting the string slip through your fingers.

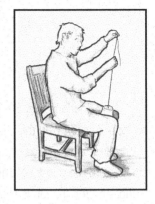

STICK FRICTION DRUM

This stick friction drum is good for making moans and groans and hiccup sounds.

PROCEDURE

Start with a clean, plastic empty container with the lid removed. Using a thumbtack, poke a small hole at the center of the bottom of the container. (If the bottom has a little button of thicker plastic at the center, poke just to the side of it.) Using a screwdriver, screw a medium-sized wood screw into the hole. Then screw it back out, leaving an enlarged hole.

On the un-pointed end of the skewer, wrap a thick collar of tape. Layer on enough tape that the collar is about one fourth inch in diameter.

Poke the skewer through the hole in the container from the inside. Slide it through so that the collar pulls up against the inside bottom. Making sure that the collar stays flush against the inside bottom, wrap a new collar on the outside, as low and flush against the plastic as you can make it, as shown in the drawing. When you're done, the collars above and below should hold the stick in place, immobilized — maybe not perfectly so, but nearly so.

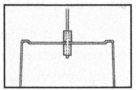

Wrap a third collar over the pointy end of the stick. This is to cover it so no one gets poked.

Cut a small piece of rag, about two inches square.

PLAYING THE STICK FRICTION DRUM

Moisten the rag with water. Hold the plastic container with one hand. With the other pinch the moistened rag around the stick between thumb and forefinger. Slide it up and down the stick to create the sounds. Try different speeds and pinching pressures to see what gives the best sound.

POTENTIAL DIFFICULTIES

Both types of friction drum are pretty dependable, but occasionally one of them does not speak readily. Violin rosin rubbed on the stick or string will often give better results. Failing that, try again with different string, stick or cloth.

FURTHER POSSIBILITIES

Bigger, more solid plastic containers produce a better sound, especially for the stick friction drums. For instance, you can make a very effective, deep-voiced, scaled-up version using a plastic bucket.

ACOUSTIC NOTES

Friction sounds, including the squeaks and groans these friction drums make, come about through a process known as stick-slip. When you slide a finger or cloth along the string or stick, it doesn't slide along smoothly, but moves instead in a rapid series of tiny jumps. These jumps create the vibration. The vibration is transmitted through the stick or string to the membrane (the bottom of the container), which acts as a soundboard.

Children can make good drums using balloon rubber for the drumhead. Balloon drums are not nearly as loud as drums with tightened heads of skin or plastic, but they do have an appealing, resonant drum tone.

The first plans on this page are for a pair of tin-can balloon drums, one smaller and one larger. Following that is a plan for a set of tubular balloon drums of varied lengths. The different tones makes the music variegated and colorful.

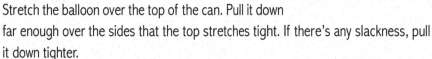

SINGLE BALLOON DRUM, SMALL

PROCEDURE

Remove the top and bottom of the can. Clean the can.

Optional: remove the paper from the side of the can.

With scissors, snip the neck part off of the balloon as shown in the drawing.

Stretch the balloon over the top of the can. Pull it down far enough over the sides that the top stretches tight. If there's any slackness, pull it down tighter.

Put a collar of one or two rubber bands around the balloon to keep it from slipping. This will be easier for two children than one: one person holds the balloon in place, another puts the rubber band on. Alternative: use adhesive tape in place of rubber bands.

Optional: add another balloon membrane to the opposite end of the can. This may make the drum a tiny bit louder, and it allows you to play on both sides if you want. You will not get two different notes this way because the acoustic interaction of the two sides causes them to produce the same pitch.

Also optional: you can improve the tone and make the drumheads longer lasting by doubling them – that is, placing a second stretched balloon over the first.

SKILL LEVEL

In making the instrument you need to stretch balloons over the ends of cans, which takes some dexterity.

MATERIALS

A mid-size tin can. 14-oz size (think of Campbell's Soup) is about right.

Large balloons. It's good to have a few on hand in case one tears.

Rubber bands.

Two unsharpened pencils, chopsticks or similar-sized sticks to use as drumsticks

TOOLS

Can opener. If available, use the pop-off style can opener (see the picture on page 2).

Scissors.

PLAYING THE BALLOON DRUMS

Sit in a chair and hold the drum between your legs. Make sure that the bottom of the drum is not blocked.

The drums can be played with fingertips or with light beaters such as chopsticks or unsharpened pencils. Use a light, bouncing-off technique rather than letting the stick or your fingers rest on the drumhead after hitting it.

SINGLE BALLOON DRUM, LARGE

PROCEDURE

The procedures are the same as those described above for the smaller can, except that the method for putting on the membrane is a little different.

The punchball comes with a rubber band attached. Remove it.

With scissors, make a single slit in the punch ball from the neck to a point short of the nub, as shown in the drawing. This allows the 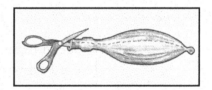 punchball to open out, more or less flat, into a sheet of rubber.

Stretch this rubber sheet over the top of the can in such a way that the nub doesn't end up in the stretched part, but is pulled over the side. Pull the sheet tight.

While you hold the stretched punch ball in place, have someone put a collar of one or two rubber bands in place to keep the punch ball from slipping. Alternative: use adhesive tape in place of the rubber band

Optional: add a second punchball drumhead to the opposite end of the can.

PLAYING THE LARGE BALLOON DRUM

See the instructions above.

TUBULAR BALLOON DRUM SET

This plan is for a set of five tube drums of different lengths. That number is arbitrary; you could just as easily make a set with just two or three drums, or as many as eight.

PROCEDURE

SKILL LEVEL

The maker cuts cardboard tubes with a hack saw, then stretches balloons over the ends of tubes.

Using the hack saw, cut the tubes to varying lengths. The exact lengths aren't important, but the following approximate lengths are suitable:

Tube 1: leave it at 2 feet.

Tube 2: 16". (Keep the leftover 8")

Tube 3: 13". (Keep the leftover 11")

Tube 4: 11" (Use the leftover from tube 3)

Tube 5: 8" (Use the leftover from tube 2).

You are going to stretch the balloon membranes over the pre-cut end of each tube (not the end that you cut). If the edges of the tube-end are sharp, the balloon may tear. Round off those edges slightly with the sandpaper.

Using scissors, snip the neck off of one of the balloons, as shown in the drawing on page 62.

Stretch the balloon over the end of one of the tubes, pulling it as far down over the sides as it will go. Usually this won't make it tight enough, so roll the edges of the balloon membrane back up the side almost to the top. Then lift it off and put it back on again, tighter this time (see the drawing). Test your tube drum by tapping it to see how it sounds, and make it tighter if necessary.

MATERIALS

Three mailing tubes, 2" in diameter and 24" long (longer is OK). Two kinds of mailing tubes are available: ones with crimped ends, and ones with straight ends and separate end-covers (see the picture on page 50). Either will work for this project, but the straight ends are preferable.

About eight large balloons. Either the 12" or 16" size will do.

Rubber bands.

Two unsharpened pencils, chopsticks, or similar-sized sticks to use as drumsticks.

TOOLS

Hacksaw.

Scissors.

Medium-grit sand paper.

Repeat this process for the remaining tubes.

Optional: double the balloon heads by putting a second stretched balloon directly over the first on each tube. This will improve the tone and allow the heads to last longer.

Use several rubber bands to strap the five tubes together in a bundle with the playing ends more or less even with each other.

TO PLAY THE TUBULAR BALLOON DRUM SET

Sit on the edge of a chair and hold the bundle of tubes between your legs, making sure that nothing is blocking the lower ends of the tubes. Play with fingers or light beaters as described above for the small tin can balloon drum.

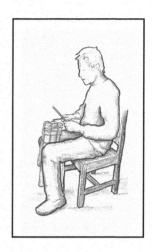

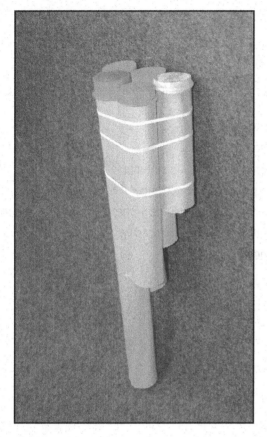

POTENTIAL PROBLEMS

Stretching the balloons over the tops of the cans or tubes may be difficult for children. The operation will go more smoothly with a helpful adult nearby.

The balloon membranes won't last forever, but they'll usually be good for a few weeks.

A very small percentage of the population is allergic to the latex used in balloons.

FURTHER POSSIBILITIES FOR BALLOON DRUMS

These drums always sound more interesting when you have several drums with contrasting tones. So if you're making tin can drums, make a few in different sizes. If you're making tubular drums, having six or eight so in the set will be more fun than having three or four. If you want to make a set much larger than about eight tube drums, they'll become hard to hold and play comfortably. In that case, consider designing a frame to hold them.

ACOUSTIC NOTES

As discussed in the acoustic notes for the bucket drums (page 42), the sound of drums is a mixture of sound from the drumhead and the resonance of the air inside. With tin can drums, we removed the bottoms of the tins before adding the balloon over the top because the drums wouldn't sound as good with the bottoms still on and the air immobilized inside. However, having the far end covered with another flexible membrane is OK because the flexibility of the second membrane allows the air inside to vibrate, and communicate its vibration to the outer air through the vibration of the membrane.

The tighter you stretch the balloon membrane, the higher its note will be. That means you can tune the drum by stretching the membrane tighter or looser. But in practice it's awfully hard to tune balloon drums with accuracy. It's probably better to just enjoy whatever tuning comes up by chance rather that trying to tune deliberately.

MAILING TUBE LUTE

The renaissance lute was a string instrument used in past centuries much like the classical guitar is used today. For people who study musical instruments, the word *lute* is also used in a broader sense to refer to instruments like guitar, banjo and violin which have a narrow neck extending out from a sound box. The mail tube lute on this page is is one more instrument that fits that description.

Is there a child in the world today who isn't familiar with the rock and roll iconography of the guitar? (Probably, but I don't know any.) The string instrument on this page doesn't have the blasting power of an electric guitar, but the form is similar and the tone, though not loud, is surprisingly good.

The simple version shown here has three tunable strings but not much of a finger board. You can finger the strings guitar-style with the left hand to change the pitches of the strings, but only in a limited way. The advanced version has a better finger board, allowing the player to do more in the way of fingering.

SKILL LEVEL

Simple version: recommended for ages 8 and up.

Advanced version: requires more dexterity; recommended for ages 10 and up.

SIMPLE VERSION

PROCEDURE

Remove the lid from the empty juice bottle and strap the bottle to the mailing tube with a rubber band going around the back of the tube as can be seen in the photograph.

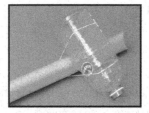

For the first string, take three of the long rubber bands and stretch them longways over and around the mailing tube and the juice bottle. If yours is a crimped-end mail tube, the inward curve of the tube end will keep the rubber bands in place. (If not, use tape or notch the tube ends to keep the rubber bands from slipping off.) When the rubber bands are in place, twist them together so that the playing portion of the rubber bands becomes like one extra-thick rubbery string. (The playing portion is the long raised section between the tube-end and the plastic bottle.)

For the second string, put two more rubber bands on and twist them into one.

For the third string, add a single additional rubber band.

MATERIALS

Cardboard mailing tube, 2" diameter by 24" long, preferably the crimped-end type (see the on page 52).

One empty plastic juice bottle, preferably the square-ish 64 fluid ounce size (common for Ocean Spray brand and similar products).

Eight 7" rubber bands (plus extras in case of breakage). These extra-long rubber bands, sometimes called "file bands," are available at office supply outlets.

TOOLS

None.

Space out the strings so that they can be played separately. If either of the twisted ones isn't twisted enough to stay together, add more twist.

PLAYING THE INSTRUMENT

First tune the rubber band strings. Do this by pulling the playing portion of each string tighter to raise the pitch. Loosen it to lower the pitch. Experiment until you have three pitches that sound good together. The thickest string should have the lowest note and the thin one the highest.

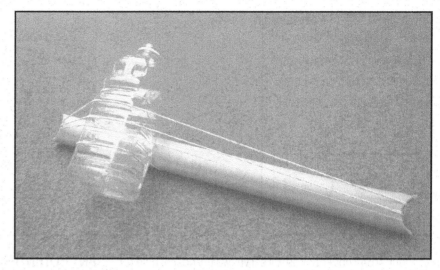

Simple Mailing Tube Lute

Strap the lute onto your body using another long rubber band (see picture, page 66). Hook it over the upper side of one crimped end, run it around your back, and hook it over the upper side of the other crimped end. This additional rubber band will hold the instrument in place like a guitar strap.

To play, pluck the strings with your right hand. With the fingers of your left hand, press the strings against the surface of the tube near the tube's end like a guitarist fretting on a guitar fingerboard. Pressing the string will produce a higher note.

ADVANCED VERSION

MATERIALS

Same as for the simple version, plus:

One more 2" mailing tube. This one should be a foot long (you may start with a longer one and cut it to one foot).

Four #64 rubber bands or similar (this is the common ¼" x 3½" size).

TOOLS

Hacksaw or carpenter's saw if needed to cut the additional mailing tube.

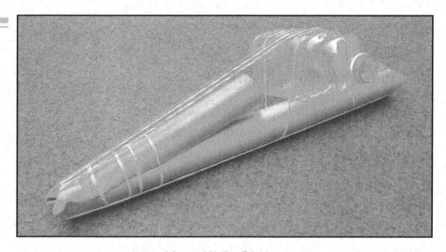

Advanced Mailing Tube Lute

PROCEDURE

Strap the juice bottle to the two-foot mailing tube as described for the simple version above.

Cut the additional mailing tube to one foot long. This tube is to serve as a fingerboard.

Squash one end of the foot-long mailing tube, as shown in the drawing. The easiest way to do his is to step on the end, flattening about four inches at the end of the tube.

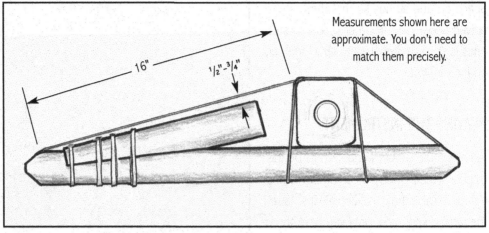

Measurements shown here are approximate. You don't need to match them precisely.

16"

1/2"-3/4"

The four #64 rubber bands will serve two purposes: holding the fingerboard in place and providing frets for playing different notes on the strings. Hold the one-foot tube in place on the main tube and bend the flattened end tube part way around the main tube as shown in the drawing. Use the four 3½" rubber bands to strap the one-foot tube in place. Position them approximately as shown in the drawing above.

Add the three strings as described previously for the simple version.

Make any adjustments needed to position the tubes, bottle and rubber band frets similar to the positioning in the drawing above.

PLAYING THE MAILING TUBE LUTE

As described above for the simple version, you can use another long rubber band to strap the instrument around your waist when you play.

The tuning and playing of this version is the same as that of the simple version, except that you can play higher notes by pressing the strings down against the fingerboard. By shifting the positions of the "frets" (the rubber bands that hold the fingerboad in place) you can tune the fretted notes. How about a boogie woogie bass line, as can be heard on the recording on the CD?

ANY POTENTIAL DIFFICULTIES?

The rubber bands, if left stretched on the instrument, will eventually deteriorate and will have to be replaced.

FURTHER POSSIBLITIES

Holding everything together with rubber bands is simple and quick, allows for needed adjustments, and makes for easy disassembly. But it's not very permanent and the components can easily slip out of position. If you wish to make things permanent once you've got everything adjusted right, use masking tape or other strong tape to fix the juice bottle and the fingerboard in place.

ACOUSTIC NOTES

Three main factors affect the pitch of a vibrating string, as illustrated in this instrument:

1) Strings vibrate faster when they're under more tension, so pulling the rubber bands tighter gives them a higher tone.

2) They also vibrate faster when they're shortened. Since pressing the string against the fingerboard makes the vibrating part of the string shorter, that too makes a higher note.

3) Heavier strings vibrate slower. That's why on this instrument the triple rubber band strings are best for low notes, while the single ones are better for higher notes.

SODA STRAW OBOE

The tone of the soda straw oboe (as you can hear on the CD) is slightly outrageous and appealing to noise-loving kids.

The instrument works on the same principals as the classical oboe, with a similar tone-producing mechanism at the mouthpiece and tone holes along the tube for controlling the pitch. It's easy to make, and a little more difficult to play.

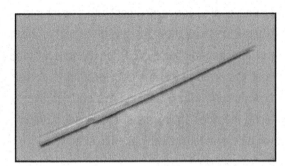

SKILL LEVEL

The instrument maker needs to make some fairly precise scissor cuts. Ages 9 and up.

MATERALS

Plastic soda straw. The best straws are fairly light and flimsy, such as inexpensive, non-name-brand straws available at the supermarket. Large, sturdy straws like those you get at fast food places are harder for children to play. Flex-straws are good because they can be bent to the optimal playing position, but non-flex straws are OK too.

TOOLS

Scissors.

Soda Straws Oboes appear in many children's instruments books and web sites. Thanks go to Robin Goodfellow, who introduced me to the idea and has used it extensively, with many interesting variations, in her work with children.

PROCEDURE

Firmly flatten about an inch at one end of the straw, making a sharp crease in each side. If the straw is a flex straw, flatten the end near the flex-portion.

With scissors, make an angle cut on each side of the flattened end, about a half inch long, as shown.

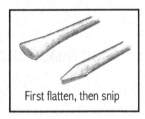

First flatten, then snip

You now have a one-note instrument! See if you can get a tone from it (see "Playing the Instrument" on the following page).

Use the hole punch to make a tone hole in the straw, positioned about 1½" from the far end of the straw. If you think of the two snips made earlier as the sides of the instrument, then the hole-punch locations should be in the top. Pinch the straw just enough to fit it halfway into the hole punch for punching at the 1½" location. Try not to make a permanent crease. Put the straw just far enough into the punch that it will punch a half-round hole. That way, when you take the straw out so that it no longer is pinched, it will open out into a complete round hole.

Play again. Practice covering and uncovering the hole with a finger as you play to get two different notes.

Repeat the operation to punch a second hole about 2½" from the far end. It's now a three-note instrument.

PLAYING THE INSTRUMENT

Play the oboe by blowing on the mouthpiece end (the flattened and snipped end). The trick is to put just enough pressure on the straw with your lips as you blow. When the pressure is right, the tone will jump out loud and clear. In addition to adjusting lip pressure, experiment with how far into your mouth you put the straw, thus changing which part of the mouthpiece portion your lips press on. Often the tone will appear when your lips press at just the right location. If air seems to just flow through without making a sound, go over the crease along the sides again, pressing hard and flattening so that it will be easier for the two halves to close.

After you've made the tone holes, bring out different notes by covering and uncovering the tone holes with your fingertips while blowing. Do your best to cover the holes completely.

ANY POTENTIAL PROBLEMS?

These instruments are fidgety, and sometimes it's hard to get a tone out of them, even for grown-ups. Since they're quick and easy to make, it won't hurt to make a few, and choose the one that plays best.

This instrument sounds quite melodic when played well, but the tuning is capricious. You cannot depend on it to produce a certain note each time you play a certain fingering.

FURTHER POSSIBILITIES

If you give the instrument a few more tone holes, you'll increase the number of notes you can produce, but you'll also make it harder for children to play. On the CD tracks 36 and 37 you can hear music played on a six-hole soda straw oboe, as well as music from the two-holed oboe described here.

Instead of using tone holes, you can make a soda straw oboe with a slide like that of a trombone. To do this, you need to find two sizes of soda straw, one of them just big enough to slide over the other. Cut the mouthpiece in the smaller one but don't give it any toneholes. Slip the bigger one on to act as the slide. In playing the slide soda straw, it's very easy to inadvertently slide the bigger straw all the way off of the smaller one. To prevent that, cut a piece of thread and tape it to the inner straw near the mouthpiece and the outer straw close to its near end. Make the thread the right length to stop the slide just before it slides all the way off.

ACOUSTIC NOTES

Instruments like saxophones, oboes and clarinets are called reed instruments because their mouthpieces use a small piece of material cut from a reed (a type of tall, woody marsh grass) to help make the sound. In the soda straw oboe the function of the reed is served by the plastic of the straw itself, with its special cutaway shape.

The reed acts as an air-gate. As the player blows and the air passes through, the reed slaps closed and springs back open in a rapid, repeated motion. As a result, the air enters the tubular part of the instrument in a very rapid series of pulses. It's this pulsing that sets up the vibration in the tube.

The column of air inside the instrument vibrates very well at certain natural frequencies. The movement of the air at one of those natural frequencies causes the reed to open and close at the same frequency. When this happens the motions of the gate and the air column work together and you get a clear tone. Covering and uncovering the tone holes changes the natural frequency of the air column, and that controls what note you get from the instrument.

BLOWN BOTTLES

SKILL LEVEL

Assembling this instrument is easy, but getting a good tone is more challenging. Recommended for ages 9 and up. Younger children can enjoy random pitches and no deliberate tuning; older children can try tuning.

MATERIALS

Several narrow-necked bottles such as soda pop bottles, soy sauce bottles or wine bottles in various sizes. Glass bottles are best (plastic ones usually don't work as well).

Optional: **Filler material** (needed only if you plan to tune the bottles). Take your choice among the following.

Water: quick & easy, gives good tone, but doesn't last due to evaporation.

Pea gravel, sand, shelled peanuts, rice, barley, etc.: these won't evaporate, but don't produce the best tone.

Plaster of Paris: permanent, gives great tone, but for working with children the fine powder is quite messy.

TOOLS

None.

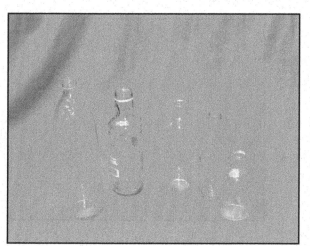

You can make a musical tone by blowing across the top of a bottle. With several bottles you can make a bottle ensemble. Getting a good tone out of a bottle takes a little practice, but many children teach themselves to do it just for fun.

Different-sized bottles make different notes, so you can get a range of pitches by using a range of bottle sizes. You can also tune a bottle by filling to varying degrees with water or other filling material.

When you have to pick up and put down a bottle for each note, it's difficult to play smooth, continuous melodies. That's why this instrument is a good one for hocketing, the playing technique in which each member of a group is responsible for just one or two notes.

For information on the group playing technique called "hocketing," see page 113.

PROCEDURE

Gather plenty of clean, empty bottles and begin blowing over the tops to test for pitch. (Read "Playing the Instrument" below for instructions on how to get the tone.)

For a random-pitch set, all you need to do is find several differently sized bottles whose notes go well together to create a your bottle set. The selection process is much like that described for glasses played by percussion on page 24.

For a deliberately tuned scale, tune by adding varying amounts of one of the filler materials suggested in the materials list on the left. The more filler you add to a bottle, the higher its pitch will be.

For more on scales & tunings, see pages 107–110.

PLAYING THE INSTRUMENT

To get a clear tone from a blown bottle, hold the bottle upright with the top against your lower lip. Purse your lips to produce a narrow,

concentrated air stream, and blow across the opening so that the air stream strikes the opposite edge of the opening. (The panpipes drawing on page 77 shows a similar technique, though with a different instrument.) The air stream must be aimed just right to bring out the tone, and it takes a little practice to get the hang of it.

If the bottles are for a single player, arrange the bottles for convenient bottle-handling on a padded surface such as a carpeted floor or a table spread with a towel.

If the bottles are for a hocketing group, then there's no need for the padded surface. Each player can hold one or two bottles in his or her hands.

FURTHER POSSIBILITIES

If the number of bottles is small you can make them easier to manage for solo playing by bundling several of them together with duct tape.

ACOUSTIC PRINCIPLES

Though these bottles don't look like flutes, the vibration is excited in a similar way. The Acoustic Notes for the panpipes on page 78 describe how blowing over the opening excites the tone in flute-like instruments.

With vessel flutes like these bottles, the size of enclosed air space is one of the factors determining the pitch. The bigger the space, the lower the note. To tune, we reduce the space inside by adding water or other filler.

Bobby Pin Styrokalimbas

...as described on the facing page.

The one on the left has bridges made from marker pens. The one on the right has wooden bridges.

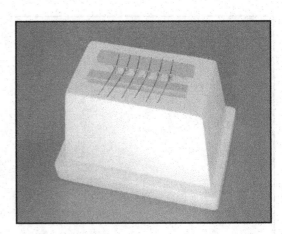

MATERIALS

for the Styrokalimba

Styrofoam picnic cooler or other large piece of styrofoam.

Bobby pins in the largest available size.

Hardware:

Six eyebolts, 2" x 8-32. (8-32 designates the shaft diameter and thread pitch. If this exact size isn't available, any similar size will do.)

Six 1" fender washers. Fender washers are large-diameter steel washers with small center holes.

Six 8-32 wing nuts to fit the eye bolts.

The bridges. For these you can use either

Wood: Two pieces about an inch square and eight inches long. (These measurements need not be precise.)

~~ or ~~

Two large felt-tip markers or similar-sized implements, about 6½" long and ¾" diameter (Marksalot and similar brands are suitable). Old, dried up ones will work just as well as new ones.

The wood will give a slightly better sound.

Adhesive for the bridges. If you use wood: white glue, Mod Podge, or hot glue. For felt markers: Mod Podge, school glue gel, or hot glue. (For adults, hot glue is quickest and easiest.)

TOOLS

Needed only if you'll be cutting wooden bridges instead of using old markers: **Hacksaw or carpenter's saw.**

Lamellaphones are instruments with sounds made by vibrating prongs. Many variants on the idea appear in southern and central Africa, where they are known by several names including kalimba, mbira and sansa. (Among people outside of Africa, they have sometimes been called "thumb pianos.")

SKILL LEVEL

Both of these instruments require small-parts assembly, and they may require one saw cut. Best for ages 11 and up.

Both of the plans on these pages use bobby pins for the prongs. Bobby pins are made of a springy steel that vibrates well. The instrument in the first plan has both a melodic and a very rhythmic quality. The instrument in the second plan is raucous, rattling, and percussive.

STYROKALIMBA

The styrokalimba uses bobby pins mounted on a Styrofoam base, attached by means of eyebolts, fender washers and wing nuts. You'll probably have to make a special trip to the hardware store to get them, but with these parts in hand the assembly is easy and requires no tools.

PROCEDURE

The styrofoam picnic cooler will be positioned upside down so that what was the bottom now becomes the top where the prongs are mounted. The prongs are to be spaced an inch apart, positioned as shown in

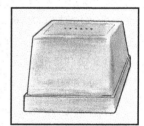

the drawing. With the cooler resting bottom-up, use the eyebolts to punch a series of six small holes in a line, an inch apart.

Place an eyebolt through each of the six holes with the eye above and a fender washer and wing nut beneath. Don't tighten yet.

If you'll be using wood pieces for the bridges, cut the two pieces of wood, each about an inch square and eight inches long. If two felt tip markers, you can use them just as they are.

 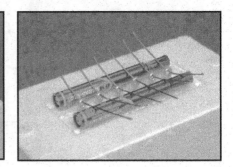

Place the bridge pieces (wood or felt-tips) on the styrofoam as shown above. Glue them in place with a suitable adhesive.

Unbend six bobby pins so that they end up more or less straight (they don't need to be perfectly straight).

Insert a bobby pin across one bridge, through the first eye-bolt, and across the opposite bridge. Tighten the wing nut from underneath so that it pulls the bobby pin down against the bridges and flexes it down a little bit at the center. Do the same for the other five bobby pins and eye bolts.

Pluck the ends of the bobby pins overhanging on each side of the bridges. If any of them rattle, tighten them down a bit more with the wing nuts.

Now you have a choice: enjoy the random scale as is, or tune the prongs to a scale of your choosing. The longer the prong (the greater length that overhangs the bridge), the lower the note it makes. Tuning is done by sliding the prongs back or forward on the bridges and through the eyebolt to vary the overhang length. It may help to loosen the wing nut for sliding, and re-tighten after. An important caveat: you can only tune the prongs on one side of the bridges. That's because if you were to tune one side and then tune the other, the tuning on side two would undo the tuning already done on side one. So, tune one side, and let the other be random. The potential range (the musical distance from the highest and lowest notes you can get) is quite large.

For most children it will be easiest and most fun to tune by ear to whatever scale appeals to them without attempting to match any pre-existing scale. They can adjust and re-tune at any time.

For more on scales & tunings, see pages 107–110.

PLAYING THE STYROKALIMBA

Pluck the prongs to create rhythms and melodies.

FURTHER POSSIBILITIES

This instrument could be redesigned to have more prongs covering a large musical range.

ACOUSTICS NOTES

The vibrating prongs, being small and thin, don't have enough surface area to move much air when they vibrate. In this they're like musical strings. So, as with string instruments, they need to be attached to a soundboard. The styrofoam makes an excellent soundboard, providing the needed surface area to project the sound out into the air.

As with any vibrating body, the faster the prong vibrates the higher the note it makes. Two factors effect how fast each prong vibrates when you pluck it: 1) Rigidity. The more rigid, the faster the vibration and the higher the note. 2). The weight and leverage of the vibrating part of the prong. This relates to how far the prong overhangs the bridge: the longer the overhanging part, the lower the note. We can't control the rigidity of the bobby pins, but we can control the overhanging length, so that's how we tune.

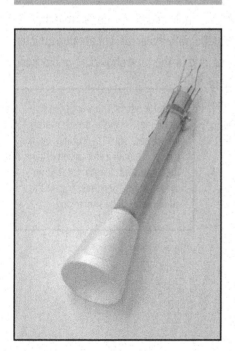

RATTELAM

This instrument makes buzzing and rattling sounds, adding interest and color to any ensemble. The bobby pin prongs are mounted in a way that brings out the buzzing.

PROCEDURE

Cut the bamboo or dowel to a length of about 10". It doesn't matter if there are joints in the bamboo.

Take six bobby pins and straighten them (unbend them at the middle). If you have large and small sizes, prepare four large ones and two small ones.

Arrange the bobby pins around the end of the bamboo. Position them so that some have long overhangs extending beyond the end of the bamboo, and some have short overhangs. Use cellophane tape to hold them in place temporarily.

Slip the hose clamp over the shafts of the bobby pins as shown. Use a screwdriver to tighten it down, holding the bobby pins securely. Important: While tightening, hold the far end of the bamboo, well away from the screwdriver and hose clamp. This is to prevent hand injury if the screwdriver slips.

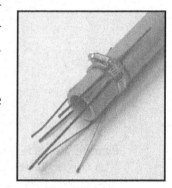

Glue the styrofoam or plastic cup on the far end of the bamboo as shown.

PLAYING THE RATTELAM

Hold the bamboo with one hand. With the other, pluck the bobby pins to make them rattle against the end of the bamboo. For a louder sound, hold the cup or the bamboo against a table top or other surface while plucking. For a two-handed playing technique, seat yourself and hold the bamboo between your legs, bobby pins up, in a way that leaves both the bobby pins and the cup untouched. Pluck with both hands.

To get different sound you can loosen the hose clamp, rearrange the bobby pins with different overhanging lengths, and retighten.

PANPIPES

A set of panpipes is a group of several tubes joined together side by side. Each tube makes one note, and together they make a scale. They're played by blowing over the open ends to get a flute-like tone. The technique is similar to blowing over the top of a pop bottle, but because the panpipe tubes are compact and easy to hold, you can play melodies by shifting rapidly from tube to tube. With their exotic, breathy sound, instruments of this sort appear in many parts of the world, from South America to Europe to South Pacific islands.

Two different panpipe sets are described here. One is made of bamboo and has all the beauty of the natural material. Because bamboo is not uniform, the measurements given in the plan cannot guarantee accurate tuning. If you make this version, plan to accept some randomness in the tuning. (With more work, adults can fine-tune the instrument by ear.)

The other panpipe set is made from tubes of PVC plastic. This set can be accurately tuned just by following the measurements in the plan. You can make the instrument without raising sawdust or fumes from the PVC if you use a rotary tubing cutter to cut the tubes (see page 2 for a picture of this tool).

SKILL LEVEL

Bamboo panpipes: These require measuring and fairly easy saw cuts.

PVC panpipes: These call for accurate measurement. The cutting with the rotary tubing cutter is not difficult.

For playing both types, it takes a little practice to get a clear tone.

Recommended for ages 10 and up.

BAMBOO PANPIPES

MATERIALS

Bamboo, about 6 feet, about 5/8" to ¾" in diameter. Available at many plant nurseries and garden supply stores.

Packaging tape or duct tape, 2" wide (this is the standard width for packaging tape and duct tape).

TOOLS

Hacksaw.

Sand paper.

Ruler or measuring tape.

The sawing will be easier for children if the tubes are held in a **vise or clamp** for cutting.

PROCEDURE

With the hack saw, cut the eight bamboo tubes as indicated below. Cut so that there's a joint in the bamboo blocking one end of the tube, with the actual cut about a quarter inch beyond the middle of this joint. The other end of the tube should be unblocked, and there should be no joints in the middle of the tube. The given lengths are only approximate, so it's not necessary to cut with precision.

Note for adults who want precision in tuning: To make an accurately tuned set, start by cutting each pipe to a length a little greater than the indicated length for the intended note. Then bring it up to the intended pitch by shortening.

Note	Length (inches)	Length (cm)
G4	8¾"	21.5cm
A4	7½"	18.5cm
C5	6"	14.5cm
D5	5⅜"	13cm
E5	4¾"	11.5cm
G5	4"	9.5cm
A5	3⅞"	8.5cm
C6	3"	7cm

For more on scales & tunings, see pages 107–110.

Round off the newly cut edges with sandpaper. To do this, lay the sandpaper on a flat surface and draw the edges of the bamboo across it with a rounding-over motion. Try to make the edges even and splinter-free.

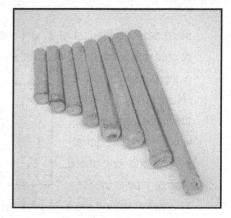

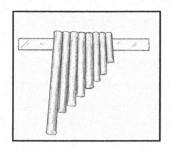

Tape the tubes together in a row. To do this, pull off a 12" length of packaging tape. Lay it on a flat surface, sticky side up. Temporarily weight the ends with a pair of jars, bowls, or anything else convenient. Position the bamboo pieces across it in order from longest to shortest with their open ends lined up evenly, as shown at left. Remove the weights and wrap the tape around the bamboo tubes. Add more tape as needed to hold them securely.

PLAYING THE INSTRUMENT

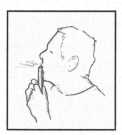

Hold the panpipes vertically in front of your mouth, so that the rim of one of the pipes touches just below your lower lip. Purse your lips and blow a narrow air stream across the pipe's rim opposite. It will take a little practice, but when you get it just right, you'll hear a clear tone. Then again, you don't have to go for that clear tone — a less focused, breathy panpipe tone can be very attractive too.

Play different notes by shifting which pipe you blow over.

PVC PANPIPES

By following this plan you can make a well tuned panpipe set without having to do any tuning by ear; you just need to cut to the lengths given in the plan.

In the bamboo pipes described above, we took advantage of the natural joints in the bamboo to form the blockage at one end of the tubes. In the plastic pipes we'll use several layers of electrician's tape for that purpose.

PROCEDURE

Measure, mark and cut the six tubes using the rotary tubing cutter. The lengths are given in the chart.

To provide the tubes with one stopped end, you'll use multiple layers of electrician's tape wrapped over the end. Snip off about 3" of electrician's tape and place it tautly over one end of one of the tubes as shown in the drawing (next page). Add another

PVC Panpipe Lengths		
Note	Length (inches)	Length (cm)
C4	13¹/₈"	33.3
D4	11⁵/₈"	29.6
E4	10³/₈"	26.3
G4	8¾"	22.3
A4	7¹³/₁₆"	9.9
C5	6³/₈"	16.3

piece crossing the first at a right angle. Add two more at 45 degree angles to the others, and keep going until you've got eight layers on there. (Multiple layers makes the wall of tape solider, which helps the tone.) Finally, add one more strip of tape in the form

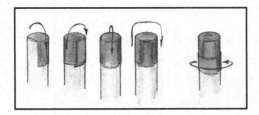

of a collar around the tube covering the ends of the pieces already in place. This ensures their adherence to the side of the bamboo and improves the appearance.

Follow the same steps to make the stopped ends for the remaining tubes.

Use packaging tape or duct tape to tape the tubes together in a row. To do this, pull off a 12" length of tape. Lay it on a flat surface, sticky side up, and weight the ends with a pair of jars, bowls, or anything else convenient. Position the pipes across it in sequence from longest to shortest with their open ends lined up evenly. Remove the weights and wrap the tape around the tubes. Add more tape as needed to hold the tubes securely.

PLAYING THE INSTRUMENT

Same as for the bamboo panpipes described on page 77.

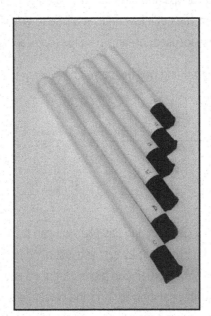

FURTHER POSSIBILITIES

The plastic pipes are tuned to a pentatonic (five-note) scale built on C. To make a complete major scale (seven tones instead of 5) add two more pipes at $9^5/_{16}$" (23.7cm) and $6^9/_{16}$" (16.7cm). You can add still more pipes for other scales or for a larger range.

The bamboo pipes are nominally tuned to the same pentatonic scale, but probably not accurately. For them too you can add more pipes for a more complete scale or larger range.

Panpipes are almost always arranged in scale-wise order,

from longest to shortest. But they don't have to be – you can position your pipes in any sequence you wish. Arranging them in other sequences allows for unusual patterns of notes.

Instead of attaching with tape, these pipes can be held together in other ways. Many traditional panpipes are held in place by binding with cord to a cross-piece. The pipes can also be glued together using hot glue or another suitable filler/adhesive.

ANY POTENTIAL DIFFICULTIES?

Even though the PVC panpipes can be made without generating dust or fumes, you might not like the idea of mouth contact with the PVC plastic. Avoid saliva contact with the plastic. Those who wish to avoid plastics altogether should make the bamboo panpipes rather than the plastic ones.

ACOUSTIC NOTES

Each pipe in the panpipe set is like a flute with no tone holes, so it only makes one note.

In flutes, the sound comes about when the player blows over the edge of a hole in the tube. In panpipes, that hole is the open end of the tube. (In some other flutes, like the bamboo flute on page 90, the blow hole is a hole in the side of the tube.) When the air rushes over the edge, it sets up eddying air currents that direct more air into the tube, then more air out of the tube, in rapid alternation. This alternation sets up the vibration in the air enclosed in the tube.

Meanwhile, the column of air in the tube has a natural frequency at which it can vibrate best. When you get a good tone from the flute, that means that the in-and-out frequency of the eddying air flow has come into agreement with the natural frequency of the air column and the two effects are reinforcing one another.

PACKING TAPE DRUMS

You can make drumheads using packing tape stretched tightly and layered across the top of the drum. It works best on drums bodies of about six inches in diameter up to ten inches or more.

For the body of the drum you can use any rigid tubular material that is open at both ends and has a large enough diameter. The plan presented here uses large-diameter cardboard tubing.

BIG CARDBOARD DRUM

MATERIALS

Heavy cardboard tube, 8" diameter by 1' long. These tubes are sold at hardware stores and lumber yards as forms for concrete pillars. The most popular brand name is Sonotube. The tubing is sold by the foot, and since whatever amount you buy will have to be cut anyway, you can probably get the yard attendant at the store to pre-cut yours to one-foot lengths.

Alternative: To make several drums in varying lengths, get different lengths anywhere from six inches to two feet.

Clear packaging tape, 2" wide. This tape is available in different weights, from thin and light to thick and sturdy. For this purpose, heavier weight is better.

Two small beaters. Try a pair of unsharpened pencils, or shish kebob skewers with cork heads.

For more on mallets & beaters: see pages 104–106.

TOOLS

None if your tubing is pre-cut.

If you have to do the cut, you need a **carpenter's saw, masking or similar tape, measuring tape and a marker.**

PROCEDURE

If you need to cut the tube, follow these steps which will help you make a good, square cut.

SKILL LEVEL

Ages 9 and up if the heavy cardboard tube comes ready-cut. The only challenge then is stretching the tape. If the tube isn't ready cut, then it will probably take two people to cut it — one to hold and one to cut.

Using the measuring tape, mark off a length of one foot. Don't make just one mark; instead, make a series of marks spaced a couple of inches apart going all the way around the tube.

Wrap a ring of masking tape around the tube following the marks.

Use the saw to make the cut, using the edge of the masking tape as a guide and following it as closely as possible.

Choose the flattest, smoothest end to serve as the one the drumhead will go over. Whether you get the tube pre-cut or cut it yourself, the edges on this end will probably need to be cleaned up. Use medium-grit sandpaper to smooth over the edge. Sanding along the inside edge will cause any loose material to separate and fall off. At the same time, try to level any jags or irregularities in the cut surface.

To form the drum head, several strips of packing tape will be stretched across the opening on the chosen end. The best sound comes about

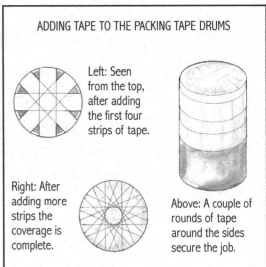

ADDING TAPE TO THE PACKING TAPE DRUMS

Left: Seen from the top, after adding the first four strips of tape.

Right: After adding more strips the coverage is complete.

Above: A couple of rounds of tape around the sides secure the job.

when the tape is applied evenly. The following is a procedure for applying the tape with minimum wrinkling and maximum uniformity, as Ilustrated above.

Tear off a strip of tape about 18" long. Lay it flat loosely across the tube opening with about five inches overhanging at each end. Flatten down one end of the tape along the side of the tube so it sticks there firmly. Grasp and raise the other end near where it crosses the opposite edge of the tube. Use both hands, with a thumb and forefinger on each side of the tape. Stretch the tape taut, pulling in such a way that the tape stays flat with minimal wrinkling, centered over the opening. Press the free end of the tape down over the side of the tube so that it adheres there. Even with this technique some wrinkling will occur; that's OK. Press down the sides again to make sure the tape is very well stuck on.

Add a second strip perpendicular to the first. Lift it up and away a bit before stretching so that the strip being added doesn't stick to the one already in place before it's pulled taut. After that one is in place, add two more strips at 45 degree angles to the first two. Continue adding strips until the whole opening at the top of the drum is covered, being sure that there are no little triangles of open space left near the edges. Remember to press all of them firmly down against the side of the tube.

Add a couple of additional rings of tape around the sides of the tube to keep the tape well in place. Place one ring near the top, and another lower where it covers most of the tape ends.

Gently press the tape down flat all over the drumhead surface, so that there are no loose ridges of tape sticking up.

PLAYING THE PACKING TAPE DRUMS

Hold the drum in a way that leaves the opening opposite the head free and unblocked. One convenient way is to sit in a chair holding the drum between your knees.

You can play with light sticks such as unsharpened pencils or shish kabob skewers with corks. Use a light touch, making sure that the drumsticks bounce off the drum head in the moment of hitting, rather than resting on the head and damping its vibration. Strike very near the edge for a higher-pitched tone. Strike about a third of the way in from the rim for a fuller, deeper tone. Don't play too hard — doing so doesn't sound any better and shortens the life of the drumhead.

ANY POTENTIAL PROBLEMS WITH THESE DRUMS?

A drumhead made of packing tape holds up well for a week or so if not played hard. When it begins to give out, it can be removed and replaced.

ACOUSTIC NOTES

The criss-cross way of adding the layers of tape makes the drumhead thicker at the center than at the edges. That arrangement — with more weight at the center and more flexibility near the edges — helps create a better tone. (Some professional drums, such as tablas, are deliberately weighted at the center.)

For information on how tubes of different lengths affect the tone, see the acoustic notes for the balloon tube drums (page 65).

MUSICAL GLASSES

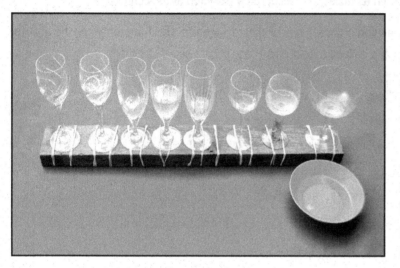

Most wine glasses produce a luminous, sustained tone if you rub the rim just the right way with a moistened finger. You can create tuned sets of glasses either by selecting glasses that naturally have the pitches you want, or by tuning the glasses. Tuning is done by adding water.

To get a tone from a single glass, steady the glass with one hand while stroking the rim with the other. For playing more than one glass, another way must be found to hold the glasses steady. In the plan that follows, the glasses are held in place with rubber bands on a board.

PROCEDURE

Put rubber bands around your board, two rubber bands for each glass you expect to use, spaced a few inches apart. If the rubber bands are too big to fit snugly over the board, double them to make them fit tight.

Fix your glasses on the board by slipping the base of each glass under a rubber band on each side as shown in the drawing.

You may enjoy the random tuning of your empty glasses. Alternatively, if you want to tune to different notes, you can do so by adding water to the glasses: the more water, the lower the note.

Place an extra glass or bowl filled with water nearby. This is the dipping glass for finger-moistening while playing.

For more on choosing among random-pitch sounds, see page 108.

For more on scales & tunings, see pages 107–110.

SKILL LEVEL

The glasses are easy to assemble, but the instrument is suitable for older and more responsible kids because the glasses are fragile and playing technique is delicate.

MATERIALS

Several wine glasses. If you have different shapes and sizes, they will give different pitches. If they're all the same, you can still get different pitches by water-tuning.

2x4 or similar board, about three feet long.

Rubber bands.

TOOLS

None.

PLAYING THE INSTRUMENT

Moisten a finger. Run the finger lightly around the rim of a glass to produce the tone. Re-moisten as necessary. If you're not getting a tone, try a slightly lighter or slightly firmer touch. If still no tone, see the notes below under potential difficulties.

ANY POTENTIAL DIFFICULTIES?

Some types of glass sing effortlessly, while others scarcely produce a tone. Hard water (high mineral content) works better than soft water. If you're not getting good results, try different glasses or water from a different source.

FURTHER POSSIBILITIES

With a large number of glasses you can make complete scales over a large range.

Players using large numbers of glasses usually mount them in several rows on a table or plywood board. This makes it possible to have a larger number of glasses within reach.

ACOUSTIC PRINCIPLES

Although the sound and the playing technique are different, musical glasses produce their tone through the same patterns of vibration as bells. Like bells, the glasses can also be played by striking the sides (very gently) with very light beaters such as chopsticks.

For an explanation of how the water tuning works, see the Acoustic Notes for the floating bowl bells on page 20.

The instruments on this page, sometimes affectionately known as Oom-Pa Tubes, are wind instruments with a unique system for setting up the vibration.

The first form of the instrument given here has a slide mechanism, allowing it to be played trombone-style. The second form has tone holes and the player creates melodies by covering and uncovering the holes as on a flute.

There are many ways to make membraerophones. The designs here are based on a clever instrument made in years past by children on the Indonesian island of Sumatra (and perhaps elsewhere too) for sale to tourists.

The name for these instruments, "membraerophones," was coined by Fran Holland, a great proponent of instrument making for children. The name reflects the fact that these instruments are aerophones (wind instruments) which use a membrane (balloon latex). The nickname "Oom Pah Tubes" comes from Robin Goodfellow's Crunch and Toodle, Puff and Sputter Band, which used them in a recent concert.

MEMBRAEROPHONE-BONE

(Mailing tube with slide, also known as Oom Tube)

This version of the membraerophone uses mailing tubes of two sizes to form a trombone-like sliding system.

PROCEDURE

With the hack saw, cut a 4" length from the fat mailing tube (the 2½" one). Put the remainder of that tube aside for later use.

Drill a ¼" hole in the side of the 4" section at the midpoint, 2" from each end.

This next step requires good attention. You're going to wrap a collar made of multiple layers of tape around the narrower mailing tube just thick enough so that the short, fat tube cut previously will slide over it snug and air-tight. The collar is located with its far side 4" from one end of the narrow tube, as shown in the drawing. If the tape you are using is fairly thin, as with masking tape or electrician's tape, it will take many wraps to build up enough thickness. Begin wrapping with the tape and keep going around and around until you've built up a collar that looks thick enough that it will fit snugly inside the short fat tube. Stop wrapping and cut the tape there. Now try slipping the short fat tube over the collar. If it fits snugly and you

SKILL LEVEL

The mailing tubes are to be cut with a hack saw and drilled with an electric drill (easier than drilling wood, but still more suitable for older kids).

MATERIALS

2" cardboard mailing tube, 2' long.

2½" cardboard mailing tube, 2' long.

The type of mailing tubes with straight ends (not crimped) is preferable (see the photo on page 52 if you're not sure what's crimped and what's not). Available at stationary and office supply outlets.

Large balloon. The 16" diameter size is best. Have an extra balloon or two on hand in case one tears.

Rubber band.

Poster-hanging tape, electrician's tape, or masking tape.

TOOLS

Hacksaw.

Scissors.

Hand drill and ¼" bit.

Clamp or vise to hold tubes for cutting and drilling.

have to force it just a little bit, that's perfect! If the collar is too big, peel back and cut off a small amount of tape and try the fit again. If the collar isn't thick enough, add more tape.

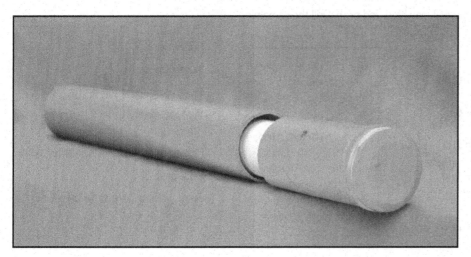

When you've got a good fit, position the short, fat tube over the collar so that the long narrower tube sticks out just about 1/16" beyond the end of the short tube.

Use scissors to snip the narrow neck portion from the balloon. Pull the balloon down over the sides of the short fat tube so that it makes something like a tiny drumhead over the protruding 2" tube end. Roll the sides of the balloon part way back up the sides of the short fat tube, exposing the hole drilled earlier. If this drumhead gets loose, remove the partly rolled up balloon and put it back on tighter. When you've got a good fit, flat but not overly tight, put a rubber band around the balloon over the outer tube to hold it in place.

You now have a one-note wind instrument. (You can test it for sound, following the instructions under "Playing the Instrument" below.) The next step will be to add the trombone-like slide. The remaining portion of the 2½" mailing tube will serve as the outer sliding tube.

To get the fit between the main tube and outer sliding tube, add another collar of tape like that described above. This collar will be at the far end of the main tube. Begin wrapping the tape at the end and keep adding layers until the collar is thick enough that the outer tube will just fit over it. This time, don't go for a tight fit — it should be just barely snug but not so tight that the outer tube can't slide easily. When you've got the fit about right, slide the outer tube over the collar and all the way up so that it bucks up against the short fat tube at the mouthpiece end.

PLAYING THE INSTRUMENT

Put your mouth over the hole in the 4" tube and blow. (Don't blow over it as with a flute; put your lips up against it and blow firmly through.) Do you get a clear tone? If not, try some adjustments to the balloon: Make sure the longer, inner tube is sticking out just a little beyond the end of the short fat tube so that the balloon stretches over the end of the inner tube. The balloon membrane should not be slack, but it should not be overly tight either. Try adjusting the amount the inner tube sticks out if the tone isn't good. You can also try stretching the balloon a little looser or tighter.

When you're getting a good tone, try the slide, extending the larger tube outward so that the instrument becomes longer. This will lower the tone. The range is limited, but the sound is great.

MEMBRAEROPHONE-TONE

(smaller version with tone holes, also known as Paa Tubes.)

This form of the membraerophone has tone holes along the side of the tube similar to those on a recorder or flute. The pitch is wobbly and undependable, but children love this instrument because the tone is strong and clear.

The instrument is given in two versions. One is of bamboo, requiring two sizes of bamboo. The other is made from PVC plastic. The plastic version is more dependable and a little easier to make, but it requires cutting and drilling the PVC — something some will prefer to avoid due to the dust and fumes.

SKILL LEVEL

Bamboo version: This version requires cutting bamboo with a hack saw and drilling with an electric drill.

PVC version: This also involves cutting and drilling, and requires a breathing mask and goggles.

Both are suitable for older kids, ages 13 and up, or for younger kids if an adult performs some of tasks.

Bamboo Version

PROCEDURE

Cut a section from the narrower bamboo, open at both ends and with no joints in it. Go for the longest piece you can get between the joints — at least nine inches long; preferably ten or eleven. Cut the ends as square and even as you can, then use the sand paper to smooth and round over the outside edges.

Mark the hole positions for the four tone holes in a row along the side of the tube at the locations indicated below. Secure the tube with a clamp or vise, and use the nail or center punch to tap a slight indentation at each location. (This will prevent the drill bit from wandering as you start the hole.) With the ¼" bit in the drill, drill the first hole. Use high drilling speed but light pressure, especially as you come close to the end of the hole; otherwise the drill may bind and grab. Drill the remaining three holes the same way.

Hole #4	2" from the tube end
Hole #3	3½" from the tube end
Hole #2	4⅛" from the tube end
Hole #1	5½" from the tube end

The exact hole locations are not important, and these locations are only suggestions.

If one end of the bamboo is not very round, measure the hole locations from that not-so-round end, leaving the rounder end for the mouthpiece.

Use the hack saw to cut a 3½" length of the thicker bamboo with no joints in it. Make the cuts as straight

MATERIALS

Bamboo, two sizes:

Between ¾" and 1" outside diameter. You will need one section 9" or longer with no joints in it.

Between 1⅛" and 1⅜" outside diameter. One short section (3½") with no joints in it.

For both pieces, the bamboo should be reasonably round in cross section, at least at one end.

Balloon, 12" size or larger.

Masking tape or electrician's tape (the standard ¾" width is good).

Rubber band.

TOOLS

Hacksaw.

Sand paper.

Electric drill and ¼" bit.

Vise or clamp to hold the material during cutting and drilling operations.

Hammer and center-punch or large nail.

Scissors.

Ruler, yardstick or tape measure.

as possible and clean up after with sandpaper or file, smoothing and rounding over the cut edges.

There will be a blow hole 1³/₄" from one end of this tube. Mark and punch the location for the blow hole. Secure the tube with a clamp or vise, and drill the blow hole with the ¼" bit.

Now you're going to wrap a collar made of multiple layers of tape around the long, narrow bamboo tube, just thick enough so that the thicker bamboo piece will slide over it snug and air-tight. The location of the far side of this collar is 3½" from the hole-less end of the tube, as shown in the drawing. Begin wrapping with the masking tape or electrician's tape, and keep going around until you've built up a collar that looks just thick enough that it will fit snugly inside the larger tube. Stop there and cut the tape. Try slipping the larger tube over the collar. If it fits snugly and you have to force it just a little bit, that's perfect. If the collar is too big, peel back and cut off a small amount of tape and try again. If the collar isn't thick enough for a snug fit, add more tape.

When you've got a good fit, slide the thicker tube over the collar to where the longer, narrower tube sticks out about 1/16" beyond the end of the thicker tube. Rotate the outer tube so that the blow hole is 90 degrees off axis from the tone holes.

Use scissors to snip the narrow neck portion from the balloon. Pull the balloon down over the thicker bamboo section so that it makes something like a tiny drumhead over the protruding end of the narrower tube, and roll the sides of the balloon partway back up the sides of the thicker tube to expose the blow hole. If the little drumhead gets loose, remove the partly rolled-up balloon and put it back on tighter. When you've got a good fit, flat but not overly tight, put a rubber band like a collar around the balloon to hold it in place.

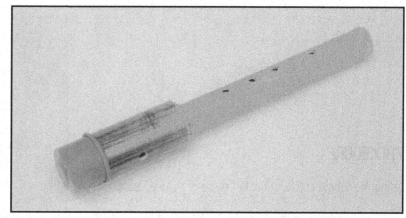

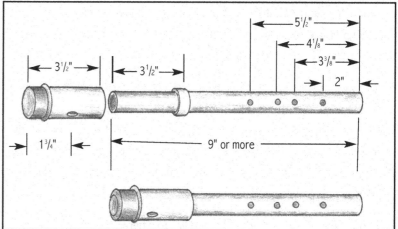

PLAYING THE INSTRUMENT

Blow through the blow hole. (Don't blow over it like with a flute; put your lips up against it and blow firmly through.) If you don't get a clear tone, try making some adjustments to the balloon: Make sure the balloon membrane is neither too tight nor too loose over the tube end. Check that the narrower tube is sticking out just a little beyond the end of the thicker one so that the balloon stretches evenly over the end of it. Try blowing again.

Sometimes the adhesive tape collar does not fit air tight and air leaks out around it. This can happen if either bamboo piece is far out of round. In that case, wrap the whole collar area with an outer mantle of tape to seal the leak.

When you've got a good tone, play the instrument by holding it to one side like a flute, covering and uncovering the tone holes with your fingers as you blow. The fingering diagram on the right shows you which fingerings work best.

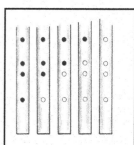

Fingerings for five notes. The blackened circles represent holes to be covered by fingers.

PVC Version

PROCEDURE

Using the tubing cutter, cut a 12" piece of ½" PVC tube.

Drill four toneholes in the 12" tube as described above for the bamboo version of the instrument. As with the bamboo, the holes can be positioned 2", 3⅜", 4⅛" and 5½" from one end (precision in these locations isn't crucial). Remember to wear the mask and goggles.

Now to wrap a collar made of multiple layers of tape around the ½" tube. Position the far side of the collar 3" from one end as shown in the drawing below. Make it just thick enough so that one side of the ¾" T-joint will slide over it snug and air-tight. The procedure is the same as that described for the bamboo version on the previous page. Wrap until you get a good fit as described in the procedures for the bamboo version.

Slide one side of the T-joint over the collar to where the ½" tube sticks out about ¹⁄₁₆" through the opposite side of the T-joint. Rotate the T-joint so that the third opening of the T is 90 degrees off axis from the tone holes.

Use scissors to snip the narrow neck portion from the balloon. Pull the balloon down over T-joint where the ½" tube is just barely sticking out, so that it makes something like a tiny drumhead over the ½" tube end. Stretch it smooth, roll the sides up a little as described in the procedures for the bamboo version.

MATERIALS

½" PVC tubing, 12". PCV tubing is inexpensive and widely available at hardware stores. (This is not the same as the acrylic plastics sold at places like Tap Plastics.) The ½" diameter is nominal: for the tubing sold as ½" tubing, the actual inside diameter is slightly larger than ½", while the outside diameter is about 7/8".

T-joint for ¾" PVC tubing. (That's right, we're calling for the ¾" T-joint, even though the tubing you're using is ½".)

Large balloon (12" size or larger).

Masking tape or electrician's tape. The standard ¾" width is good.

Rubber band.

TOOLS

Rotary tubing cutter. See the picture on page 2 if you don't know this tool.

Electric drill and ¼" bit.

Vise or clamp to hold the tubing during cutting and drilling operations.

Hammer and center-punch or large nail.

Scissors.

Ruler, yardstick or tape measure

Pencil or pen.

Breathing mask and goggles to use while drilling the PVC. Inexpensive goggles and throwaway breathing masks are available in hardware stores.

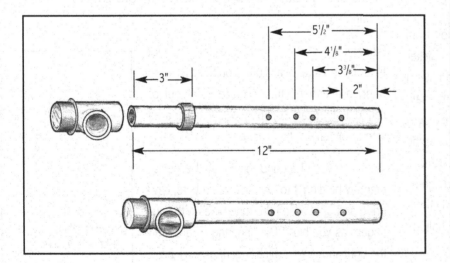

PLAYING THE INSTRUMENT

In this version, the blow hole is the opening in the T-joint to the side of the main tube. Blowing through this hole, the instrument can be played as described above for the bamboo version.

ANY POTENTIAL DIFFICULTIES?

Do not let children attempt to drill bamboo or plastic tubing without first securing the tube with a vise or clamp. The bit has a way of suddenly biting into the material and spinning the tube along with it.

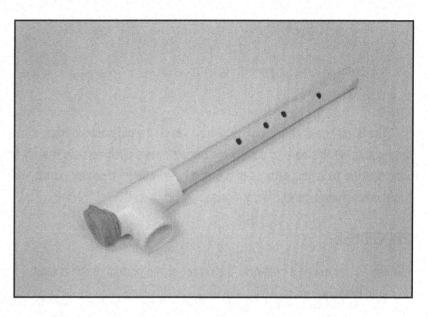

When you complete either the bamboo or the PVC version of the membraerophone-tone, you'll be impressed with how clear and melodic it sounds. Naturally you'll think how nicely it could work as a well tuned wind instrument for use in an ensemble. Be forewarned that these instruments are very wobbly in pitch! You can't depend on them to play in tune.

If you're considering making the PVC version, remember that drilling the PVC raises toxic dust and fumes. Wear the breathing mask and goggles. You may also be wary of mouth contact with PVC. The side hole in the T-joint is large enough that you can press the area round your lips against the rim of the hole for blowing, avoiding direct oral contact.

FURTHER POSSIBILITIES

You can make these instruments longer for lower pitch, and add more toneholes for a wider range of notes.

ACOUSTIC NOTES

These membraerophones function like reed instruments, even though they don't use actual reeds. As described in the Acoustic Notes for the Soda Straw Oboes (page 70), the essential element in reed instruments is something that functions as an air gate, converting the steady stream of the player's breath into a series of rapid pulses. Here's what's happening inside the membraerophones: When you blow into the shorter, thicker tube, there's no place for the air to go except to squeeze under the balloon and escape into the longer, narrower tube. But the balloon membrane doesn't just lift up and let the air through in a steady stream; instead it repeatedly lifts and closes back down, letting air through in a series of quick little puffs. It's the rapid pulsing of these puffs of air that sets up the vibration in the narrrow tube.

The longer the tube is, the lower the note it produces. You can easily see this happening in the membraerophone-bone with its slide. When you slide the outer tube outward, making the tube longer, the sounding note gets lower. In the tone-holes version of the instrument, something similar is happening but less obviously. When all the holes are covered with fingers, the full length of the tube is in play. But when you uncover one or more of the holes, this creates leaks along the side of the tube. It's as if you are making the tube shorter, and the sounding note gets higher.

BUCKET BASS

The bucket bass on this page is a variation on the old washtub bass, also known as a gutbucket. It's hard to control the bucket bass's pitch very accurately, but the tone has the satisfying fatness of a string bass. With its rhythmic punch, it's good for bands playing bouncy, dancy music.

PROCEDURE

Use the ¼" bit to drill a hole near the center of the bottom of the bucket.

Cut the broomstick or other stick to 40" long (several inches longer for an adult player; a few inches shorter for a small child).

Use the saw to cut a notch in one end of the broom stick as shown. The notch should be wide enough to fit the cord.

Notches cut at opposite ends of the stick, perpendicular to each other.

At the other end of the stick, make a similar notch, but oriented perpendicular to the first notch.

Cut a piece of cord about four feet long.

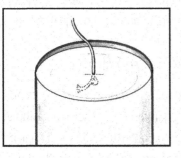

Make a large knot in one end of the cord, and then run the other end through the hole in the bucket from the inside. Pull it through so that the knot pulls up against the bottom of the bucket on the inside.

Place the bucket on the floor bottom-up so that the cord comes up through the hole. Plant one foot firmly on the bucket to hold it in place, then position the stick vertically so that one of the notches rests over the bucket-bottom's rim. Pull the string over the notch in the top of the stick. Angle the stick slightly over the bucket so that you get the shortest possible string length between the bucket and the point where the string crosses the notch. Mark this point in the string by holding it pinched between your fingers. Take away the stick, and tie a heavy knot in the cord at that point.

Bring the stick back and see if you got the knot position right: when you pull the string up and over so that the knot catches behind the notch, the string should be more or less taut. If the string is loose and floppy, the instrument won't work well. If necessary, untie the knot and try again. When you've got it right, the instrument is done.

SKILL LEVEL

The bucket bass calls for one hole drilled with an electric drill, as well as very dextrous hand saw work . Best for ages 13 and up.

MATERIALS

One large, heavy plastic bucket, the bigger the better. The five gallon buckets often used as containers for commercial or industrial products work well. The bottom of the bucket must have a ridge or raised rim around its periphery (not all buckets have this).

Four to six feet of heavy cord. Nylon cord about 3/16" in diameter is ideal, but anything between about 1/8" and ¼" will be OK.

An old broom stick or other stick of similar size. Either square or round in cross section is OK.

A block of wood, a thick book, or anything similar that can be used as a spacer.

TOOLS

Scissors to cut the cord.

A drill and ¼" bit.

Hacksaw.

PLAYING THE BUCKET BASS

First, get the instrument together: With the bucket upside down, the string coming through the hole in what's now the top, place a block of wood, book, or similar spacer under the rim to hold one

side a little off the floor. Standing to one side of the bucket relative to the block, place one foot on the edge of the bucket over the block. Put the stick in position, with the lower notch in place over the rim of the bucket-bottom opposite the side where the block is. Hook the cord over the stick's upper notch so that the knot catches behind the notch. Now you're ready to play.

Pluck the string strongly (no need to be delicate about it). As you do so, pull the stick to the side to increase the tension on the string, using your foot to brace the bucket against the tension. The more you angle the stick, the greater the tension and the higher the note.

The gutbucket provides a nice, rhythmic bass. Varying the tension to get different notes makes it all the more lively. When you get good at it, you will be able to play somewhat in tune with other music.

FURTHER POSSIBILITIES

To avoid having to place the block under the rim of the bucket, an adult can cut a sound hole about four inches in diameter in the side of the bucket. Then the bucket can rest flat on the ground, and there's still an opening for the sound.

If you use a real washtub or other very large container instead of the bucket, the bass will be louder.

ACOUSTIC NOTES

The block under the rim of the bucket is to provide a "soundhole" for the air inside the bucket. With the bucket flat on the floor, the air inside is trapped and the sound isn't as good.

It's difficult to control string pitch very accurately by varying the tension. That's why relatively few instruments work this way and most string instruments use other means for controlling the pitch.

Two simple flutes are described here. One is made of bamboo, the other of PVC plastic tubing. These flutes can play in both the upper and lower registers, for a range of a little under two octaves.

From a nature-lover's perspective the bamboo is much more pleasing, of course! Its disadvantage is that bamboo dimensions are varied and unpredictable. For that reason, it's impossible to specify in advance the dimensions for a well tuned flute. For those interested in making a more refined version of the bamboo instrument, the Acoustic Notes section below has instructions for fine-tuning through hole sizing and placement.

With the plastic flute, if you follow the prescribed lengths and placements, you'll get a flute that is, for the most part, well tuned. (Due to acoustic limitations, tuning is never perfect throughout the range in a simple flute like this). The disadvantage is that drilling the plastic raises potentially toxic fumes and dust, requiring goggles and a dust mask.

For either the bamboo or the plastic flute, you can choose between two forms: a sideblown flute (comparable to the orchestral flute), or a duct flute (comparable to a recorder). I recommend the duct flute because it requires only a bit more effort to make, but it's far easier to play for anyone without training in flute playing.

BAMBOO FLUTE

PROCEDURE

Cut a section of bamboo to 12" long with a node blocking at one end, as shown in the drawing on the facing page. The distance from the center of the joint to the open end of the tube opposite should be 11".

Round off the newly cut edges with sand paper.

On this bamboo tube, mark the locations given on the facing page for the blow hole and the six tone holes. Use a hammer and a center punch or nail to tap a small indentation at each of the hole locations. Place the tube in a vise or, if no vise is available, clamp it to a table. Tighten securely, but not enough to crack the bamboo. With the drill and 5/16" bit, drill the blow hole and six tone holes. Keep firm control of the drill while drilling and be careful not to break through suddenly, plowing into the opposite inside of the bamboo and damaging it.

HOLE LOCATIONS

Blow hole:

¾" from the middle of the bamboo joint as observed from the outside.

Tone holes:

Hole Number	Distance from the open end		Pitch
1	6¹¹/₁₆"	(17cm)	B
2	5¹³/₁₆"	(14.8cm)	A
3	4¹⁵/₁₆"	(12.5cm)	G
4	3⅞"	(9.8cm)	F
5	3⅛"	(8.0cm)	E
6	2"	(5.0cm)	D
End of tube	0"	(0cm)	C

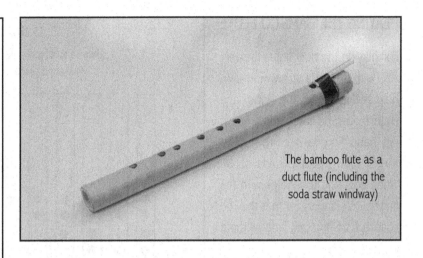

The bamboo flute as a duct flute (including the soda straw windway)

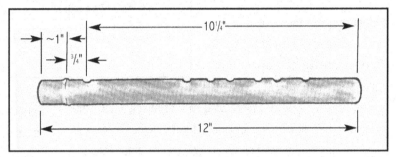

Use the threaded rod to clean up the holes. Slide it in and out of the holes to break away any splinters and smooth the edges. Then slide it into the bamboo from the open end and scrape to clean inside and remove any burrs. If you don't

The bamboo flute as a sideblown flute (no windway has been added).

have a threaded rod, use a screw or bolt, cleaning as best you can from outside the hole.

The instrument is now playable as a side-blown flute. For instructions on playing it that way, see "Playing the Instrument"

below. However, it will be much easier to play as a duct flute. To complete the instrument as a duct flute, read on.

With scissors, cut a section of plastic soda straw two inches long. Squash one end flat, firmly enough that it remains somewhat squashed.

Cut 4" of electrician's tape. Tape the straw onto the bamboo

just at the edge of the blowhole as shown in the photo. By angling the tape backward a bit, make it so that the straw angles slightly down toward the blowhole, and will direct its air at the far edge of the hole. Make the tape just tight enough to hold the straw semi-squashed, leaving a narrow opening to create a focused stream of air.

The windway

Now try sounding the flute. Cover all the holes with fingers and blow into the straw, first softly and then a little harder. Blowing softly, you should hear a quiet low note. When you blow a little harder, it should jump to a louder, higher note. If it doesn't produce a clear tone, make sure all the holes are well covered. Also, also try uncovering some of the farthest holes to see if other notes work better. If it still doesn't sound clearly, adjust the soda straw angle, placement, or the narrowness of the squashed opening, and try again. It may take a few tries to get these adjustments right and bring out the tone.

PLAYING THE BAMBOO FLUTE

For playing the duct flute (the version with the soda straw windway), hold the flute with the right hand fingers over the lowest three holes, left hand fingers over the upper three. Blow into the soda straw. When covering toneholes with the fingers, it's important that they be covered completely and without leaks.

Fingerings for the tones of a C major scale are given at right. This flute is capable of playing in two registers. The lower register is the series of tones you get by playing with relatively light wind pressure. By following the fingerings for the higher notes and playing with greater wind pressure, you can continue that series of notes into the upper register.

The tones of the upper register sound an octave above those of the lower register. However, on a simple flute like this they tend to be slightly flat (meaning, they sound a little lower than their ideal pitch). You can correct this by increasing wind pressure to raise the pitch of flat notes.

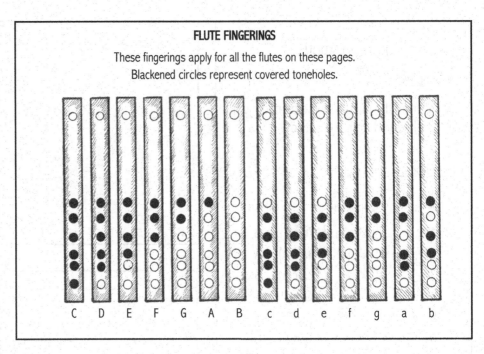

FLUTE FINGERINGS

These fingerings apply for all the flutes on these pages.
Blackened circles represent covered toneholes.

C D E F G A B c d e f g a b

Without the soda straw windway, you can play the instrument as a sideblown flute. Hold the flute with the left and right hand fingers over the holes as described above, but with the flute extending horizontally to the right. Position the blow hole in front of and just below your mouth. Form a narrow windway by pursing your lips slightly, and blow against the far edge of the blowhole. Getting a clear tone this way requires practice. Fingerings for the sideblown version are the same as for the duct flute.

PVC FLUTE

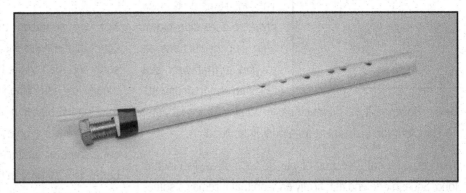

PROCEDURE

Using the tubing cutter, cut a 12½" section of the ½" plastic pipe.

On this tube, mark the locations given in the box on the facing page for the blow hole and the six tone holes. Use a hammer and a center punch or nail to tap a small indentation at each hole location. Place the tube in a vise or, if no vise is available, clamp it to a table. Don the dust mask and goggles. With the drill and 5/16" bit, drill the blow hole and six tone holes. Keep firm control of the drill while drilling.

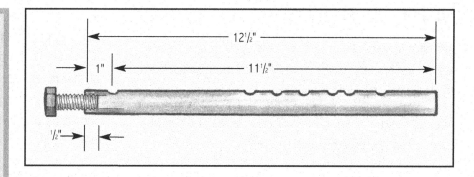

½" PVC tubing, 12½". This tubing is available in hardware stores. (It is not the same as the acrylic plastics sold at places like Tap Plastics.) In the tubing sold as ½" the actual inside diameter is a bit larger than ½" and the outside diameter larger still.

5/8" bolt, shortest available length. 1½" length is OK and widely available; 1" or less is better.

Plastic soda straw.

Electrician's tape.

Rotary tubing cutter (see photo, page 2).

Electric drill and 5/16" bit.

C-clamp or bench vise.

Pliers or vise grips.

Scissors.

Hammer and center punch or large nai.l

Breathing mask and goggles. Throw-away breathing masks and inexpensive goggles are available at hardware stores.)

Optional: **Threaded rod**, 12" or longer, any diameter.

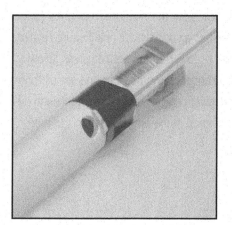

Use a threaded rod, screw or bolt to clean up the holes as described on page 93 for the bamboo flute.

The flute needs a stopper at the blowhole end. (The plastic doesn't have a natural blockage there as the bamboo flute does.) Force-thread the 5/8" bolt into the end of the tube. With luck it will fit snugly, and forcing it to thread its way in will probably require pliers or vise grips. If the fit is not snug, wrap a layer or two of cellophane tape over the bolt threads and try again. Thread it ½" into the tube.

For those with the skill to do so, the instrument is now playable as a side-blown flute. For instructions on playing it that way, see "Playing the Bamboo Flute" on page 94. However, the instrument will be much easier to play if you complete it as a duct flute. Procedures for attaching a piece of soda straw for this purpose are the same as those for the bamboo flute as given on page 93.

HOLE LOCATIONS

Blow hole:

    1" from one end of the tube.

Tone holes

Hole Number	Distance from the end opposite the blow hole		Pitch
1	6⅝"	(16.8cm)	B
2	5⅝"	(14.3cm)	A
3	4¹¹/₁₆"	(11.9cm)	G
4	3¹¹/₁₆"	(9.4cm)	F
5	3⅛"	(8.0cm)	E
6	2"	(5.0cm)	D
End of tube	0"	(0cm)	C

PLAYING THE PVC FLUTE

The playing techniques and fingerings for the plastic flute are the same as those for the bamboo flute as described on page 94.

Adjusting the positioning of the bolt (screwing it in further or out more) affects the tuning and playability, so if you like playing this instrument but you think its tuning or tone could be improved, you may experiment with the bolt adjustment to find whereit works best.

ANY POTENTIAL PROBLEMS?

The pitch of simple flutes such as these tends to vary depending on how hard the player blows. With practice you will learn to play in tune by controlling wind pressure.

In the PVC version, the drilling will raise fumes and dust. Be sure to wear the breather and goggles.

FURTHER POSSIBILITIES

Due to unpredictable variations in the dimensions of bamboo, it's likely that a flute made according to the bamboo plan will be at least a little out of tune, and possibly a lot. By taking a different approach you can make a well tuned instrument, but it takes more effort and skill. This work is more suitable for adults than children, and for beginning flute makers it will probably take a few tries to get the tuning right. Here are notes to help you in the process. The principles described here can also help you if you wish to make a flute tuned to a different scale.

The tuning of the lowest note (the all-toneholes-covered note) depends on the distance from the blowhole to the end of the flute. To make this note lower, make the flute longer; for higher make the flute shorter.

For the higher notes (those with one or more toneholes open), the main factors are the size and placement of the first open hole of the fingering for the note in question (see the fingering chart). Making the hole larger or placing it closer to the blowhole raises the pitch; smaller or farther lowers the pitch.

Here's a sensible approach to fine-tuning for the bamboo flute, following those principles.

Start by cutting the tube and making the blowhole, but make the tube a little longer than the recommended length. Without toneholes added yet, this flute will play only

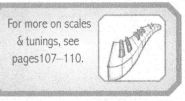

For more on scales & tunings, see pages 107–110.

the lowest note (the "all toneholes covered" note). Check the pitch of that note. Since the tube is too long, it should be a little too low. Shorten the tube bit by bit, checking the pitch at each step, until the note is right.

Now add the tone holes. Space them as indicated in the chart on the preceding page above, but make the holes initially too small, say 5/32" in diameter.

Check the pitch at the lowest hole (that is, with all but the farthest hole covered). Since the hole is small, the pitch should be too low. Using larger and larger drill bits, enlarge it until the pitch is right.

Repeat the process for the remaining holes.

If you make one of the holes too large and the resulting pitch is too high, lower it by covering over a small part of the hole with heavy adhesive tape or thickly painting nail polish around the rim and inside.

ACOUSTIC NOTES

Though they use slightly different systems, both the side blown versions and the duct flute versions of the flute produce their tones by an air stream over the edge of a hole in the tube. The edgetone effect is discussed in the Acoustic Notes for the panpipes plan on page 78.

There are a few words about how tone holes work near the end of the Acoustic Notes for the membraerophones (page 89). The bamboo flute has a special additional feature relating to tone holes: the use of lower and upper registers, allowing the player to get two ranges of notes from one set of toneholes. The upper and lower registers come about through different patterns of vibration in the air enclosed in the tube.

Here are two string instruments that use fishing line for strings. They're more challenging to build than the rubber-band string instruments on pages 7 and 64, but they have advantages: they're more dependably tunable, they have a larger musical range, they can be played in more sophisticated ways, and they're louder.

Two different zither forms are given here. One has twelve strings and is played simply by plucking the strings. The other has three strings played with a slide like a lap steel guitar. Both of them use a peculiar styro-soundboard arrangement that gives them a unique tone and makes them surprisingly loud compared to most unamplified string instruments.

DIDDLEY BOW (3-string board zither played with a slide)

The name I've used for this instrument — diddley bow — is one of the traditional names for board zithers played with a slide in earlier times by slaves and their descendents in the southern U.S. Several important early blues and R&B players got their start playing diddley bows.

MATERIALS

2x4 board, any kind of wood, 24" long. (Nominal 2x4, which is actually a little less than four inches wide, is OK.)

Monofiliment nylon fishing line, 40 lb. test strength. (Other strengths will also work, but the tunings given here are calibrated for the 40 lb. test. Avoid very lightweight fishing line, which doesn't sound as good.) Fishing line is available at hardware stores and sporting goods stores.

Three medium-small nails, about 1½" long

One large nail or bolt. The ideal size is 3½" long by ¼" or more in diameter. Any similar size will do.

Three eye bolts, 2½", 8-32. (2½" is the total length. 8-32 refers to the shaft diameter and thread pitch. This is a commonly available size. Eyebolts of other dimensions might do as well, as long as they are close to this size. The size of the eye itself is not important.) Available at hardware stores.

Styrofoam picnic cooler or other large piece of styrofoam. If you can intercept a used piece on its way to the landfill, grab it. New picnic coolers are available at many supermarkets, large pharmacies. Any size will do but larger will be louder.

About 6 extra-long rubber bands. Seven-inch rubber bands are sold at stationary stores and office supply outlets, sometimes under the name "file bands."

Something to use as a slide. Try a small bottle or jar, a large and heavy bolt, the head of a wrench or pliers ... anything smooth, hard and heavy will work. Alternatively, stainless steel guitar slides are available for $5 or $6 at music stores.

TOOLS

Carpenter's saw.

Electric drill and 11/64" bit.

Scissors.

Tape measure or yardstick.

Opaque felt-tip marker such as Sharpie.

Electronic keyboard, electric tuner, or other instrument to tune to.

PROCEDURE

Cut the 2x4 to 24"

Choose which side of the board is the better side (nicer looking), and mark two lines across the board on this side, 1" from each end. On one of these lines, mark three points: one at the center and one on each side 1" away from the center point.

Using the 11/64" bit, drill through the board at each of these three points. These holes will hold the eyebolts that are to be used for tuning.

A special feature of this instrument is fret markings. These are like the frets on a guitar, except that while a guitar uses raised frets, this instrument needs only markings to show where to position the slide to get the notes you want. Starting from the line where you just drilled the holes, use the felt marker to make lines across the board at the locations shown in the chart on the right.

At the end opposite the eyebolt holes, on the end of the board (not on the top surface), mark three points spaced like the three holes you drilled earlier: one at the center, and two more spaced an inch to each side.

Drive a small nail into each of these points, pounded in to where the nail stands about a half inch above the surface.

Screw an eyebolt into each of the holes you drilled. To get some turning leverage and make it easy to thread the bolts down, insert a large nail or the shaft of a screwdriver through the eye of the eyebolt and use it to turn the eyebolt. To get it started, you'll probably have to force the eyebolt in quite firmly as you start turning. Screw it down to where the top of the eyebolt stands about 1½" above the wood surface.

Cut three pieces of nylon line, each 28" long.

Take one of the pieces of nylon line and attach it to one of the nails by knotting it with a strong knot.

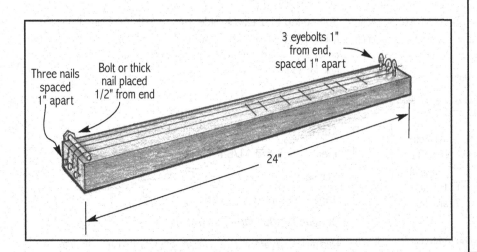

Three nails spaced 1" apart

Bolt or thick nail placed 1/2" from end

3 eyebolts 1" from end, spaced 1" apart

24"

Zithers are instruments like autoharps, hammer dulcimers and Appalachian dulcimers, as well as the instruments on these pages. For people who study musical instruments, they differ from guitars, violins and the like in that they have no separate neck.

FRET MARKER LOCATIONS

The chart shows the fret line locations for a complete chromatic scale. The numbers in bold print show the locations for the notes of a major scale. As a visual guide, make the fret marker lines for the major scale notes heavier than those for the other notes.

Fret Mark	Distance from Eyebolt Holes (inches and centimeters)	
1	1¼"	3.1cm
2	**2⅜"**	**6.1cm**
3	3½"	8.9cm
4	**4½"**	**11.5cm**
5	**5½"**	**14.0cm**
6	6⅜"	16.4cm
7	**7⅜"**	**18.6cm**
8	8⅛"	20.7cm
9	**8⅞"**	**22.7cm**
10	9⅝"	24.5cm
11	**10⅜"**	**26.3cm**
12	**11"**	**27.9cm**
13	11⅝"	29.5cm
14	**12¼"**	**30.1cm**
15	12¾"	32.4cm
16	**13¼"**	**33.7cm**
17	**13¾"**	**35.0cm**
18	14¼"	36.1cm
19	**14⅝"**	**37.2cm**

At the other end, attach the line to the corresponding eyebolt with just a bit of slack. Rather than tying to the straight shaft, tie somewhere around the eye of the eyebolt (the circular part).

Carefully begin tightening the fishing line string by turning the eyebolt clockwise, causing the string to wrap around the shaft. (Again, use a nail or screwdriver through the eye for easy tightening.) As you take up the slack and the string begins to get tight, try to have the string come off the shaft at a height of about 3/8" above the wood surface. For now, don't over tighten; just leave the line mildly taut.

Attach the other fishing line to the two remaining eyebolts and nails in the same fashion.

Slip a large nail, screw or bolt under the strings close to the end opposite the eyebolts. Position it about a half inch from the end.

The instrument can play as it is now, but only very quietly. The styrofoam picnic cooler will make it much louder. The cooler is to be positioned over the strings, with one edge of the cooler resting directly on the strings quite close to one end as shown in the photos.

It will be held there by about six of the large rubber bands. Stretch the bands around the cooler, going across the bottom longways, up the sides and across the open top. Turn the cooler upside down and position it as shown over the strings with the long rubber bands crossing under the 2x4 to hold it in place. Peer underneath and make sure that the edge

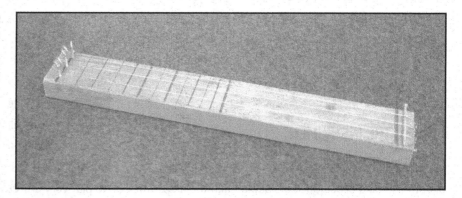

Above: the board alone.

Below: The board with styrofoam in place, and a slide alongside in the form of a small jar.

of the cooler is pressing on the strings directly over the line that you drew there earlier. If it's not positioned right, the fret markings will be out of tune.

Now you've got a good, loud instrument, and you can use the eyebolts to tune the strings to the pitches below. When tuning, keep your face averted and away from the strings in case a string snaps. Tune by comparing the notes on the zither to the notes of an electronic keyboard or other reference instrument. (The chapter on tuning, page 109, has more information on this process).

Melody string: F above middle C

High drone: F (same as melody string, not the octave below)

Low drone: middle C

When you first tighten the strings, they won't hold tunings well. You'll have to keep coming back and tuning up again. Eventually the strings will stabilize and tunings will hold better.

For more on scales & tunings, see pages 107-110.

Of course, you can try other tunings, and you can also enjoy playing the instrument in random tunings. But if you attempt to tune any of the strings much higher than about G, chances of string breakage increase.

PLAYING THE INSTRUMENT

In one hand, hold a small bottle or jar or whatever else you plan to use as a slide. Pluck the strings with the fingers of the other hand. Touch the slide to the melody string at different points along its length to get different notes. The fret markers below the strings will help you find your pitches and play in tune. Don't press down hard with the slide, because that throws off the tuning relative to the markings. Use the drone strings to fill in under the melodies. This instrument is good for glissandos and vibratos which you create through subtle movements of the slide. With practice, this allows you to play very expressively.

12-STRING FISHING-LINE ZITHER

This instrument uses almost the same materials and methods as the diddley bow. But it's configured differently and favors a very different style of music. While the diddley bow player creates melodies by using the slide to get a range of notes out of one main melody string, you create melodies on this 12-string instrument by playing from string to string.

PROCEDURE

Cut the 2x8 to 30".

Choose which side of the board is the better side (nicer looking), and mark a line across the board on this side, 1" from one end.

The eyebolts that are to serve as tuning pins will be located at different distances from this line, allowing the strings to be different lengths, as shown in the drawing and chart on the facing page. Mark the twelve eyebolt locations on your board.

Using the 11/64" bit, drill through the board at these twelve points.

Beyond your 1" line, on the end of the board (not on the top surface), mark twelve points spaced 1/2" apart. The first should be ¾" from the left edge, next at 1¼", then 1¾", etc. (These are the same distances from the left side of the board as on the chart on the following page.)

Drive a small nail into each of these points, pounded in to where the nail stands about a half inch above the end surface.

Screw an eyebolt into each of the twelve holes you drilled previously. Screw it down

EYEBOLT HOLE LOCATIONS

Hole Number	Distance from the 1" line (Inches or centimeters)		Distance from left side of board (Inches or centimeters)		String Pitch
1	28"	71cm	6¼"	15.9cm	C
2	25"	63cm	5"	14.6cm	D
3	22½"	57cm	5¼"	13.3cm	E
4	21"	53.5cm	4¾"	12.1cm	F
5	18¾"	47.5cm	4¼"	10.8cm	G
6	16¾"	42.5cm	3¾"	9.5cm	A
7	15"	38cm	3¼"	8.3cm	B
8	14"	35.5cm	2¾"	7cm	c
9	12½"	31.5cm	2¼"	5.7cm	d
10	11¼"	28.5cm	1¾"	4.4cm	e
11	10½"	26.5cm	1¼"	3.2cm	f
12	9¼"	23.5cm	¾"	2cm	g

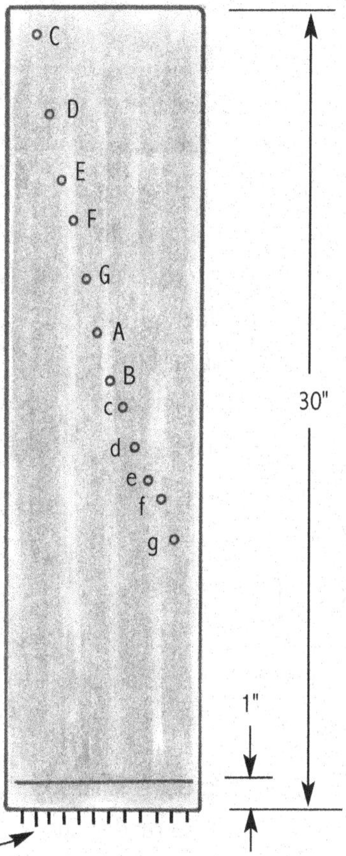

C
D
E
F
G
A
B
c
d
e
f
g

30"

1"

12 nails spaced 1/2"apart

to where the top of the eyebolt stands about 1½" above the wood surface. To make it easy to thread the bolts down, insert a large nail or the shaft of a screwdriver through the eye and use it for turning.

Cut a piece of nylon line 34" long, and attach it to the first end-nail. For good attachment, knot it several times.

At the other end, attach the line to the corresponding eyebolt. Rather than tying to the straight shaft, tie anywhere around the circumference of the eye.

Carefully tighten the line by turning the eyebolt clockwise, causing the line to wrap around the shaft. As you take up the slack and the line begins to get tight,

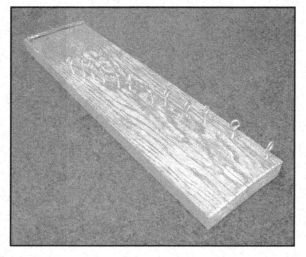

The board before adding the styrofoam.

try to have the line come off the shaft at a height of about 3/8" above the wood surface. For now don't over tighten; just take up the slack and leave the line mildly taut.

Attach the remaining eleven lines in the same fashion. For each one, start by cutting a piece of nylon line about 6" longer than the distance from its nail to its eyebolt.

Slip the 8" bolt or rod under the strings about halfway between the 1" line and the end of the board.

The styrofoam picnic cooler will be positioned over the strings, with one edge of the cooler resting on the strings quite close to the end. Look at the photo to see the configuration, and follow the instructions near the end of the previous plan (page 99) for putting the cooler in place with long rubber bands.

The strings can now be tuned to the notes indicated in the chart on the previous page. Use the eyebolts to tune the strings to these notes. Tune by comparing the notes on the zither to the notes of an electronic keyboard or other reference instrument. (The chapter on tuning, page 109, has more information on this process).

For more on scales & tunings, see pages 107–110

When you first tighten the strings, they won't hold tunings well and you'll have to retune frequently. Eventually the strings will stabilize and their tunings will hold better.

You can try tunings other than that suggested above, or enjoy playing the instrument in random tunings. But if you attempt to tune any of the strings much higher than the note given for it in the chart, chances of breakage are high.

PLAYING THE 12-STRING ZITHER

Pluck the strings with the fingers of both hands. Optionally, you can also use a slide on any of the strings, as described for the diddley bow plan above.

ANY POTENTIAL PROBLEMS?

The configuration with the styrofoam resting on the strings is unbeatable for getting good volume out of the strings, but it's not very portable. Read the section on "Further Possibilities" below for alternative suggestions.

The rim of the styrofoam will eventually break up a little at the point where it rests on the strings. See "Further Possibilities" below for a modification that will alleviate this problem and at the same time improve the sound.

FURTHER POSSIBILILITIES

To reinforce the rim of the styrofoam where it crosses the strings, add a piece of threaded rod long enough to span the width of the wooden board. It can be held in place with hot glue or other non-runny adhesive. This piece will contact the strings and eliminate wear on the styrofoam. It will also affect the sound, slightly reducing the loudness but providing a clearer tone quality.

Without the styrofoam these wire zithers are too quiet to be heard well. Are there other ways to make them louder? Here are a couple of alternatives to try.

1) Simply rest the board, without the styrofoam, on a table. Some tables work fairly well as soundboards. Or try a suitcase with rigid sides, or an old wooden trunk.

2) Place a styrofoam cooler upside down on the floor or on a table, and rest the board zither on top of it.

FOUND-OBJECT PERCUSSION

Many everyday objects have the potential to make musical sounds. Several of these appear in plans in this book, for example, empty tin cans and jars as tuned percussion are described on pages 5 and 24, and hair combs to serve as rasps are described on page 21. On this page are additional ideas for found-object instruments.

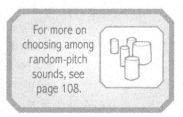

For more on mallets & beaters: see pages 104–106.

Metal Pots and Pans

Pots and pans, struck with light beaters, are the stuff of every child's kitchen drum set. Try out as many different pans as you can find, and choose those that sound best. Thin-walled pots usually sound better than thick ones or ones with heavy coatings. Strike each pot or pan in different places a to see which striking points sound best, and try different sorts of beaters. Place them on a carpet or a towel rather than resting on a hard surface. Deep pots and mixing bowls may sound good in the regular upright position, struck on the side. Other pots sound best inverted and struck on the bottom. In that position, it helps to have an air opening below, rather than resting the pan flat on its rim so that the air inside is trapped. Some pot lids work nicely too, but they usually don't ring well while resting flat on a surface; they do better suspended by a string. The same goes for broiling pan trays and other large, flat forms.

Glass and Ceramic Pans and Bowls

The comments above for pots and pans apply here.

Many glass or ceramic pans are also good for finger-squeaking. Wet your fingers or put a tiny bit of water in the bottom and practice rhythmic squeaking with the fingertips.

Silverware and Kitchen Gadgets

Most silverware sounds best suspended by thread like chimes. Barbecue grates — some of them, in any case — contain a rainbow of different tones. Egg slicers (the kind with

tensioned wires) are awfully quiet, but some of them do make a pretty sound.

Plastic & Paper Bags, Cellophane, Bubble Wrap

In the early days of radio, cellophane-scrunching was used for the fire-burning sound effect. Nowadays some kinds of plastic bags make good crackling sounds.

Plastic and paper bags are good for popping too, as every child knows. So is bubble wrap.

From the Scrap Metal Yard and Hardware Store

You can have a wonderful time testing metal shapes with a couple different beaters in hand. Here are a few shapes that may make good sounds:

Flat sheets and disks. With thin sheet metal, hold the piece loosely by one corner and tap in different locations. To assess the sounds of thicker pieces, raise the piece, drop it, and tap it in free fall. If the sound is good, the piece can later be suspended by a cord. When suspending, try different suspension points on the object to find which gives the best sound.

Bars and pipes. Hold loosely between thumb and forefinger between a fourth and a fifth from one end and tap at the center. Or tap in free fall.

Bell shapes. These appear in the guise of steel fence-post caps, among other things. Hold at the top and tap the side.

What Else?

Furniture, cars, doors, metal lampposts, table tops … Sounding objects are all around us.

For more on choosing among random-pitch sounds, see page 108.

MALLETS & BEATERS

The words *mallet* and *beater* mean more or less the same thing, but musicians usually use "mallet." Many of the instruments described in this book call for mallets. This isn't a one-size-fits-all situation: different instruments sound good with different sorts of mallets. These pages show a variety of mallets, either readymade or easy to make, suited to instruments in the book.

The most important variables in musical instrument mallets are hardness, heaviness, and the size of the striking surface. For instance, while one sort of instrument might sound best with a small, hard, lightweight mallet, another might call for a soft, medium-heavy mallet. When trying an instrument for the first time, it's often useful to try a few different types to see what mallet works best.

WHAT KIND OF BEATER TO USE?

Small, hard beaters tend to bring out a bright or edgy quality in an instrument's sound.

If the sound you're getting from a percussion instrument seems dull and lacking definition, try using harder mallets.

Softer or larger mallets usually bring out a fuller, mellower sound.

If the sound seems too edgy, go for something a little softer.

USING PADDING TO GET JUST THE RIGHT HARDNESS

To make mallets of different hardnesses, you need suitable mallet-head materials. It's not always easy to find just the right weight and hardness among commonly available materials. One trick is to start with a mallet head of material that's too hard to begin with — a metal spoon or a wooden drawer knob, for instance — and soften it by adding one or more layers of padding. Many of the mallets shown on these pages can be modified in this way.

Mole Skin is the easiest and most effective way to add padding. Mole skin is an adhesive-backed felt-like cloth sold in pharmacies as a foot-care product. Add one, two, or more layers depending on how soft you want the mallet to be.

Other materials you can use for padding:

A wrap of cloth,
A few rounds of electrician's tape,
An overlay of rubber bands.

Lightweight / Soft or Medium-hard

UNSHARPENED PENCILS

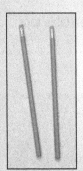

A pair of unsharpened wooden pencils works well for many light or small instruments. For a soft beater, hit with the eraser end. For harder, use the wood end.

Very lightweight / Medium-hard

CHOPSTICKS

Wooden or plastic chopsticks work well for light or small instruments. Hold at the narrow end; strike with the heavier end.

Medium lightweight / medium hard

FELT-TIP MARKERS
such as Sharpie or Marksalot

These markers, as well as other types of markers and pens, can provide a beater that's similar but  slightly heavier than pencils or chopsticks.

CORKS ON SHISH KABOB SKEWERS

Shish kabob skewers made of hard, springy wood or bamboo are available at food stores. They are pointed at one end. If you're careful about it, you can force the pointed end into a cork, not quite all the way through. Don't let children hold the cork in their hands while doing this! Place the cork on a table top and force the skewer in from above. A pair of cork beaters works well on small drums and many other medium-small instruments.

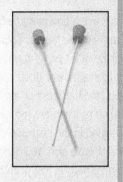

The photo shows an unmatched pair using two different kinds of corks.

LARGE NAILS, BOLTS OR SCREWS

For a couple of the very small in- strument plans in this book, the nicest sound comes from strik- ing with a suitably sized nail, bolt or screw. To protect the player's hand, wrap the pointy end with a layer of masking tape or electrician's tape.

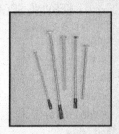

TAPE WRAP

For a larger, softer heads on the ends of pencils, chop- sticks or shish kabob skewers, add wraps of elec- trician's tape or masking tape.

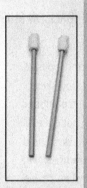

METAL SPOONS

You can hold a pair of metal spoons by the handles and strike with the bottom of the spoon-head. Occa- sionally it's also effective to strike with the edge. The metal makes an extremely hard mallet. To soften it, add one, two or three layers of mole skin to the bot- tom, depending on how soft you want to make it. (If needed, you can later remove the mole skin and clean up the spoons.)

WOODEN STIRRING SPOONS
(plastic ones too)

Wooden spoons and similar plastic ones make excellent medium-hard, medium-weight mallets just as they are. Usually it's best to strike with the side of the spoon's head. If needed to make the striking area a little softer, add layers of mole skin, electrician's tape, masking tape or duct tape.

RUBBER BAND WRAP

Twist rubber bands over one end of a pen- cil, chopstick or similar stick to build up an oval shape which will add a little weight and provide a very soft mallet head.

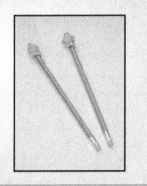

LARGE PLASTIC
SERVING SPOONS

Large plastic serving spoons can serve for wooden bars and other sound sources that require a slightly heavier beater.

SCREWDRIVER HANDLE WITH OPTIONAL PADDING LAYER

You can use a pair of screwdrivers as mallets, holding them by the blade and striking with the handle. To protect your hand from the blade, wrap the end of the blade with several rounds of masking tape, electrician's tape or duct tape. For different screwdrivers, the hardness of the handle varies. If the ones you're using are too hard to bring out the best sound in the instrument at hand, give them layers of mole skin. You don't have to layer over the entire handle; just wrap around the striking area. The mole skin can later be removed to let the screwdrivers be screwdrivers again.

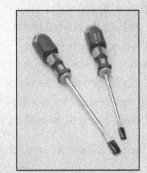

HARDWARE NUTS ON DOWEL WITH OPTIONAL OVERWRAP

If you get suitable sizes of hex nuts and wooden dowels, you can force-thread the nuts onto the dowels to form a mallet head at the end of the dowel. Two nuts positioned against one another at the end of a dowel make a mallet head of good size and weight. With a 5/16" dowel and 3/8" hex nuts, the fit is close but not snug enough. To make a snug fit, wrap the end of the dowel with a single layer of electrician's tape, then thread the nuts over that. 14" dowels are good for adults; shorter is OK for kids. With the nuts left uncovered, this makes a very hard mallet. Give them overwraps of mole skin, electrician's tape, or masking tape to mitigate the hardness. The one on the left in the photo has a moleskin overwarp; the one on the right does not.

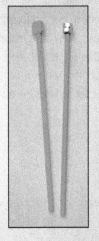

SMALL SUPERBALL ON SHISH KABOB SKEWER

If you're careful about it, you can force the pointed end if a shish kabob skewer into a high-bounce rubber ball (superball), not quite all the way through. Don't hold the ball by hand while doing this! Place the ball on a table top and force the skewer in from above. This makes an excellent all-purpose soft mallet.

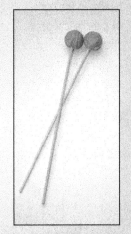

Larger superballs have many uses as well, but shish kabob skewers aren't strong enough to support them. The mounting for these usually requires pre-drilling, then inserting and gluing a dowel.

Children will be able to enjoy most of the instruments in this book even when the instruments are not tuned to recognizable scales. So you can ignore this chapter on tuning and still get a lot out of the book. But the musical possibilities are more exciting, especially for older children, when you have the option of tuning to recognizable scales.

The chapter contains two sections:

Scales. This section provides very basic information on musical scales as applied to the making of children's instruments. It also talks about the option of not tuning to any scale at all.

Practical Tuning Techniques. This section discusses the process of tuning by ear. It also coverselectronic tuners.

SCALES

IS IT NECESSARY TO TUNE TO A SCALE?

A musical scale is a set of pitches that can be used in making music. In western music, there is one standardized scale that is used nearly universally. This is the scale pianos are normally tuned to, the scale that is programmed into electronic keyboards, the scale that the guitar's fretboard is set up for, and so forth.

There are several reasons to tune your instruments to the notes of this scale. It allows you and your children to play familiar melodies. If the children make many instruments, then standardizing the tuning allows them to play in tune together. And it allows home-made instruments to play in tune with piano and guitar and other grown-up instruments.

But consider the alternative as well. Between the lowest note you can hear and the highest, there's a continuum of pitch available. Why not allow children freedom to explore this territory before locking them in to one scale?

A lot of the instrument-making projects in this book are well suited to a random-scale approach. If you're willing to listen with open ears, such scales sometimes turn out to make surprisingly lovely music. Remember that whatever scale your children come up with, by design or by chance, it is legitimate as long as someone enjoys the music it makes.

Even when children aim to replicate familiar scales, you can help keep the enjoyment rate up and the frustration rate down by not looking for precision in tuning. Tuning by ear is often difficult even for experienced adults. But if you don't demand perfection, you'll find that the ear can make musical sense of do-re-mi even when the pitches are only approximately correct.

Thus, an emphasis on perfect tuning isn't necessarily the best approach with children. Still, it's likely that you and your kids will want to do at least some deliberate tuning of your instruments, and the rest of this chapter will help with that.

SCALES AND SCALE TYPES

The standard western scale in its most complete form is the chromatic scale, technically known as 12-tone equal temperament. It has twelve notes per octave, encompassing all the notes on the piano, black and white: C, C#, D, D#, and so forth. Most pieces of music, however, do not use all twelve of these notes. Instead, typical melodies use scales of seven or fewer notes per octave. Most familiar is the seven-note (diatonic) scale known as the major scale. Also particularly important for children's instruments are five-note (pentatonic) scales.

Each of these two scale types — five-tone and seven-tone — has its advantages. The advantage of the seven-tone scales is that you can play more familiar tunes than with the five-tone scales. For instance, with the five-tone scale you can play "Mary had a Little Lamb" and "Peter, Peter, Pumpkin Eater," but not "Three Blind Mice" or "Twinkle Twinkle Little Star." With the seven-note major scale you can play all of these.

The advantage of the five-note (pentatonic) scale is that you can make good music with fewer notes and easier construction. Also, with the pentatonic it's easier for children to

MAKING RANDOM PITCHES LESS RANDOM

Finding Pleasing Scales Among Random-Pitch Objects

Many instruments in this book are made of randomly pitched sounding objects like jars or tin cans. You may not be able to control the pitches of these objects, but you can create appealing scales by selecting the ones among them that happen to sound good together.

As an example, imagine you're making the clay flower pot instrument described on page 6. The flower pots are not easily tunable, so you have to content yourself with whatever pitches your flower pots happen to make. Yet, with a reasonably large number of pots to choose from you can almost always come up with a set of tones that work well together musically.

To do this, take an intuitive approach. Tap the various pots, listen to their pitches, and look for a grouping of two or three whose tones seem to complement one another. With those pots establishing the basis for a tonality or musical mood, seek among the remaining pots for others that contribute to the musical whole. Gathering as many pots as seem to belong until you have a set that feels complete and musical. Those whose tones don't fit with the others can be put aside, or perhaps used in another grouping.

In this way, with flower pots as well as other random-pitch objects, you'll often come up with appealing scales that you might never have found if you were tuning deliberately.

play freely without hitting notes that sound like wrong notes.

You can tune to these scales, or a good approximation, without checking what you're doing against a keyboard or electronic tuner or other outside authority. Just tune by ear to whatever scale you like, and play all the melodies you want within it. If you don't intend for your instrument to play along with other instruments, this approach will work fine.

If you want to be able to play in tune with other instruments, the instruments will need to be in agreement with each other, tuned to the same notes. In that case you'll probably want to tune to standard pitches. You can do this by pitch-matching with a keyboard or other professionally made instrument, or using an electronic tuner. The process is described on the following page.

SUGGESTED SCALES FOR CHILDREN'S INSTRUMENTS

Many of the instruments in this book could be made to produce a complete chromatic scale (all twelve notes per octave). If you're ambitious, go for it! But for work with children it's often best to stick with simpler scales, making the instruments both easier to make and easier to play. In the plans for the tunable instruments in this book, two scales are suggested: a five note major scale and a seven-note major scale each built on C. They're shown here on the piano keyboard over a range of one octave.

C Major diatonic scale

The same seven notes can also function as scale known as the natural minor scale:

C Major pentatonic scale

The same five notes can also function as a minor pentatonic scale:

For greater instrumental range, any of these scales can be extended higher or lower by repeating the same pitches in higher or lower octaves. For instance, a two-octave pentatonic scale could contain these notes:

PRACTICAL TUNING TECHNIQUES

With some of the instruments in this book, you can make well tuned versions without having to tune by ear. These are the ones for which the correct tuning happens automatically when you follow measurements given in the plans. For other instruments tuning by measurement isn't feasible. With these, tuning is either up to you and your ear, or you and your electronic tuner. The remainder of this chapter explains this kind of tuning.

These tuning techniques require you to adjust the instrument's notes up or down to agree with the intended pitch. What you do to adjust the note depends on the instrument —

for example, you may need to adjust string tension, shorten a bar, or add water to a jar. The specific techniques for these pitch adjustments aren't included in the discussion below since they're different for different instruments, but they can be found in the instrument plans in this book.

The two main tuning methods are tuning by ear and using an electronic tuner. Here are the procedures.

TUNING BY EAR

Tuning by ear typically involves pitch-matching against an existing instrument whose tuning you wish to replicate. Electronic keyboards, even cheap ones, can serve this purpose well. So can a piano or even a well tuned guitar. Also, some electronic tuners include a sound function, producing an audible tone at any desired pitch, and this allows you to use them for ear tuning as well.

The idea is that you sound the desired note on the keyboard, tuner or other instrument, then play the note on the instrument you are tuning. The keyboard diagrams on these pages will help you find the notes you need on the keyboard. Listen and compare: is the note-to-be-tuned too high or too low? Adjust it as needed and compare again. Repeat until you have a satisfactory match. Do this for each of the notes you wish to tune.

Hearing whether the note-to-be-tuned is too high or too low, and by how much, is a skill. It can be particularly difficult when the tone quality of the note-to-be-tuned is very different from that of the tuning reference note. Some people have an innate ability for this kind of pitch comparison, others less so. Everyone improves with practice.

USING AN ELECTRONIC TUNER

Electronic tuners have become quite affordable in recent years, so you needn't be a music pro to own one. The idea is that you play a tone on your instrument and the tuner uses a meter or an LED display to tell you what the note is and how much it is above or below standard pitch. You adjust the note, making it lower or higher as need be (change string tension, shorten the bar, or whatever). Check the tuner again to see if you've got it right, and repeat the process until you're satisfied. You do this for each of the notes that you wish to tune.

Many electronic tuners give read-outs calibrated in cents. A cent is 1/100 of a musical semitone. Professionally tuned instruments are usually in tune to within a few cents of the ideal. You can be as much of a perfectionist as you want about this, but with children making their own instruments you don't need to be so precise. For average untrained listeners, tunings don't sound noticeably sour unless they're off by more than about 10 cents. With youngsters for whom precise tuning is difficult, 20, 25, even 30 cents off may be OK.

For some of the instruments in this book you'll have a hard time getting a clear reading from the tuner. These are either instruments whose sounds are of very short duration, or ones that have complex blends of strong overtones. For these, you'll probably have to put the tuner aside and tune by ear as described above.

Putting the Instruments to Use

Once you've made some of the instruments in this book, it will be time to put them to use. A fully developed set of musical activities for children would be beyond our scope, so I will only touch on a few possibilities here. If any of the following broad ideas seem promising, you can to develop them further to suit your purposes.

Sound Effects in Stories and Songs

With very small children, you need simple ways for engagement that don't require pre-learned musical skills. One way is through songs or stories in which the children can add suitable sounds at suitable moments. People from an earlier generation may remember songs like "Pop Goes the Weasel" with its well timed "pop!" or "Down by the Station" with its "Puff puff, toot toot!" Such songs are ready made for children to jump in at the right moment with poppers, puffers and tooters. Other suitable songs can be found or made up for the purpose. You can also invent stories to fit the sound-makers on hand. Depending on the capabilities of your children, you can keep the sound effects simple or develop them more elaborately. This activity is easily understood; it works even with very simple noisemakers, and it can be a lot of fun.

Graphic Notation Systems

A simple graphic system can help turn random noisemaking into something more organized and musical. With children ranging from little-sized to middle-sized, you can create systems to indicate who plays when, whether to play loud or soft or fast or slow, when to play pre-planned musical segments, and so forth. The system might involve color signals, shape signals, X's and O's, or hand signals. Musical sequences can be composed in advance, or they can be controlled in real time by a child or adult acting as the conductor.

Improvisation

Improvisation with kids can be greatly rewarding, but it takes some planning to carry it off successfully. The topic of improvisation is too large to treat here, but here are a few basics.

It helps to create a framework or set of rules for improvisation. This might include preplanning what instruments to use. It might include understandings about how long the piece is to last, perhaps with prescribed changes in style or instrumentation to highlight different sections of the piece. The framework might include agreements about who takes a solo when and what the other musicians do while the soloist is soloing. Small children and even many bigger ones will need schooling in awareness of the music's underlying pulse in order to play in coherent rhythm (see the sidebar on pulse and rhythm).

Here's an example of a framework for improvisation that has proven successful with small children. One child starts with a simple repeated phrase. Best are phrases of just two notes on a very simple rhythm, such as long-short-short, long-short-short, repeat. (Another good starting place: the rhythm of someone's name.) When the first child has established the pattern solidly, a second child enters on another instrument, playing an equally simple, contrasting rhythm. When these two have established a firm relationship between themselves, a third may enter with a new added pattern on another instrument.

When all the players have entered and a composite fabric has been established, the first player may change to a new pattern. The second and then the third follow with changes of their own, and the fabric continues to evolve. Over time as children become more skilled, they can try more complex patterns, as well as playing with fewer restrictions.

Call and Response

"Call and Response" is a term musicologists use for vocal music in which a leader sings a line and a separate group responds with an answering line. Typically, the leader and group go back and forth, with the leader creating variations while the responding group's line stays the same. The same kind of interaction can be done instrumentally. When they get the feel for it, the role of leader can pass from one child to another, with each child getting a turn. This form makes for a lively style of musical interaction.

PULSE AND RHYTHM

One of the basic elements of music is the beat or, to use a better term, pulse. Pulse is the steady ticking of time underlying the music. When you tap your foot along with a piece of music, you are tapping out the pulse. Even if no one happens to be tapping their foot, the pulse is there, implicit in the timing of the notes. Usually you can sense it without having to think about it.

Rhythm is related to pulse, but is different. It refers to musical patterns in time. For instance, the notes of "Mary Had a Little Lamb" come in a certain rhythm which is based on the pulse but has its own timing.

Most children relate intuitively to a musical pulse. When they play along, they instinctively keep time with the music. But this is not a sure thing; sometimes kids don't pick up on it so automatically. To enable small children to play coherently together, it helps to give them some practice with this. Here's an exercise that can help: First have them practice tapping a steady pulse. Then have one child or group play the pulse while another taps out a different rhythm over it, such as the rhythm of "Mary Had." Then do a role reversal. When you move on to call and response playing, planned improvising, or other musical activities, remind them of the importance of staying with the pulse. If suitable, give one child or group the job of tapping out a steady pulse to keep the group together while they play.

To keep the music moving briskly the players should fit their calls and responses within a steady time frame. A typical time frame might be a call that lasts for eight beats (two bars) followed by a response of the same length. (Once again, see the sidebar on pulse and rhythm.)

With children who have developed more skill, the pre-planned response can be made more elaborate, perhaps incorporating different instruments playing at different times, instruments playing in harmony, or shouts and vocalizations punctuating the instrument sounds. For added variety, you can create two or more response lines to be given at different times.

Beyond Call and Response

You can create other patterns of musical organization similar in concept to call and response but different in form. For instance, instead of exchanges between a leader and the group, exchanges can be between a leader and two groups taking turns, or multiple leaders and multiple groups with some way of signaling who goes when.

For another variation, have sections performed by the group interspersed with sections where different children do solo parts. Many ring games, handclapping games and other traditional children's song games function this way. A lot of the fun in these traditional games is the challenge of staying in time and keeping things lively, never knowing who will be called upon next.

Another format, suitable for two players, is question and answer. One person creates musical "question" phrases while another gives musical "answers." After a time, they reverse roles.

Movement

Another central element in traditional children's song games is positioning and movement — doing appropriate dance movements in place, or skipping from place to place among and around the group. Even the simplest movements can help the musical activity take shape.

Freeze dances are particularly popular with kids. One or more people play instruments, while the others dance to the music. When the music suddenly stops, the dancers must freeze where they are. It can be done competitively (the last person to freeze is eliminated after each round; the game ends when there's only one dancer left), but even without the competition it's great fun.

Hocketing

Several of the instruments in this book are well suited to the playing technique called "hocketing." Hocketing is a group-playing technique in which each player is responsible for just one or two notes. Other players are responsible for other notes. The players play in turn, one after another, to create the melody. As an example, think of bottle-tooting (getting a tone by blowing across the top of a soda pop bottle). It's easy to create a tuned set of bottles by filling them with different amounts of water, but not so easy for one person to pick bottles up and put them down fast enough to play a

melody. With the bottles distributed amongst a group of children ready to play in turn, the melody becomes possible. It takes some musical planning, but the result is an excellent group activity.

I've been speaking of melody, but a similar approach is well suited to other sorts of musical patterns too. For instance, "oom-pah-pah" accompaniments are especially easy and fun played this way.

Hocketed music has a unique spatial quality, with the sound moving around the room from player to player. You can take advantage of this in planning hocketed arrangements. Position the players in ways that reflect the patterns of the music. This makes it easier for youngsters to learn parts and perform them correctly. It also highlights the logic of the musical relationships, and brings an enjoyable, game-like interaction to the activity.

CD TRACK LISTING

You can hear the sounds of the instruments in this book on the accompanying audio CD. Here's a listing of the tracks.

1. Hello! (Children's instruments playing in ensemble.) Instruments in order of appearance: Big packing tape drums, claves, shaker, two sets of panpipes, rasp, xylophone, balloon drums, another rasp, stick friction drum, tubulon.

2. Tin Cans. The first bit heard is an improvisation on a randomly tuned set, then a tuned set playing a variation on "Twinkle Twinkle Little Star."

3. Flower Pot Bells. Two different sets appear — one plays through most of the track; the other appears briefly at the end.

4-7. Box Zithers

4. Two open cardboard box zithers

5. Two small styrofoam tray zithers

6. Two cardboard box zithers with soundboards and bridges

7. The deluxe styrofoam model playing "Jesu Joy of Man's Desiring."

8. Claves. Several different pairs playing together.

9-10. Corrugaphones

9. Blown corrugaphones, four differently tuned tubes played in sequence.

10. Whirled corrugaphones, four differently tuned tubes played in sequence and overlapping.

11. Floating Bowls. The track starts with the bottoms-up bowls. Bowl bells come next, and then a little of both. Bird calls and wind sounds are audible in the background.

12. Rasps. An ensemble of scrapers playing together.

13 - 14. Percussion Jars

13. The percussion jar set heard in this track hasn't been water-tuned, but the jars were chosen to form a scale.

14. A water-tuned set of percussion jars plays an improvisation including the folk melody "This Old Man."

15. Shakers — several of them playing together in a shaker ensemble.

16 - 22. Bar Percussion Instruments

16. Randomly tuned box wrenches

17. Bolts on styrofoam cups

18. Spoons on balloons

19. Rods on balloons

20. Bamboo woodblocks

21. Tubulon on rope followed by tubulon suspended in box

22. Xylophone

23. Bucket drums, accompanied by hand claps

24. Whirled strings — several of them heard in sequence

25. Balloonchords. The track starts with the balloonchord zither, followed by the balloons-alone-chord with bridges, and finally the balloons-alone-chord without bridges.

26-31. Plosive Aerophones

26. Golf tubes (accompanied by duct flute) playing "The Minstrel Boy."

27. Corrugated plastic tubes, first scraped and later side-struck.

28. End-slapped mailing tubes — two sets playing a duet.

29: Cardboard stamping tubes

30. Cardboard end-struck tubes

31. Large PVC stamping tubes accompanied by sandpaper and bamboo percussion.

32. Friction Drums. A string friction drum appears first on this track, soon joined by a stick friction drum.

33-34. Balloon Drums

33. Tin can balloon drums with added percussion

34: Tubular balloon drum set with added percussion

35. Mailing Tube Lute

36-37. Soda Straw Oboes.

36. The simple two-hole version

37. A six-hole soda straw oboe. "Scotland the Brave," performed by Robin Goodfellow.

38-39. Blown Bottles

38. A small selection of bottles, untuned. (The percussion sound is the bottles themsleves being clinked together between blown notes.)

39. A larger selection of bottles, water-tuned.

40-41. Lamellaphones

40. Styrokalimba. The track starts with a styrokalimba with felt-marker bridges. Soon it's joined by one with wooden bridges, tuned very high. Two short pieces are heard, the second of which has added percussion (sandpaper and claves).

41. Rattelam. A demonstration of goofy sounds.

42. Panpipes. First on the track is a short passage played on bamboo panpipes, then a longer piece played on PVC panpipes.

43. Packaging Tape Drums. Two 8" diameter cardboard drums of different lengths with drumheads of layered packaging tape.

44. Musical Glasses

45. Membraerophones. On this track the membraerophone-bone is heard first, soon joined by the membraerophone-tone.

46. Bucket Bass, joined by a styrofoam kalimba.

47-49. Flutes

49. Bamboo Flute. Robin Goodfellow performs "Skye Boat Song."

50. PVC Flute. Robin Goodfellow performs "Country Garden."

51. PVC Flute joined by membraerophones. Robin Goodfellow plays "Louis Augustine."

50-52. Fishing Line Zithers

50. Fishing Line Diddley Bow plays a raggy "Three Blind Mice."

51. 12-String Fishing Line Zither without bridge.

52. 12-String Fishing Line Zither with a bridge.

53. Goodbye! (Children's instruments playing in ensemble.) Instruments in order of appearance: Tubulon, claves, two sets of panpipes, shaker, big packing tape drums, balloon-alone-chord, xylophone.

ABOUT THE AUTHOR

Bart Hopkin is maker of acoustic musical instruments and student of instruments worldwide. He earned a B.A. magna cum laude from Harvard University in folklore and mythology specializing in ethnomusicology in 1974, and later received a B.A. in music education and a teaching credential at San Francisco State University.

In the following years he worked as a high school music teacher. Several of those years were at a public secondary school and the government-run music school in Kingston, Jamaica. There, in addition to teaching, he researched and wrote on Jamaican children's songs.

From 1985 to 1999, Bart edited the quarterly journal *Experimental Musical Instruments*. Since 1994, he has written several books on instruments and their construction, including the leading resource, *Musical Instrument Design* published by See Sharp Press. He has produced CDs featuring the work of innovative instrument makers, including the highly successful *Gravikords, Whirlies & Pyrophones* from Ellipsis Arts publishers. He has taught musical instrument construction at the School of the Art Institute of Chicago, presented talks at the Acoustical Society of America, the American Academy of Arts and Sciences, the Center for Computer Research in Music and Acoustics at Stanford University, and Media Lab at MIT, and has consulted and presented workshops at the Exploratorium science museum in San Francisco.

THIS BOOK WAS CREATED BY

EXPERIMENTAL MUSICAL INSTRUMENTS

Experimental Musical Instruments is an organization devoted to interesting and unusual musical instruments, be they newly invented, traditional, or historic and half-forgotten. Some of our books, journals and CDs present fascinating instruments, instrument makers, and music from around the world. Others provide how-to information for designing and building instruments, including both exotic and familiar types. Experimental Musical Instruments also carries hardware items for instrument making, such as tuning gears and zither pins, fret wire, and electric pickups.

To find out more about Experimental Musical Instruments and what we have available, please visit our web site or contact us to request a catalog.

EXPERIMENTAL MUSICAL INSTRUMENTS

PO Box 421, Point Reyes Station CA 94956, USA
Email emi@windworld.com   http://www.windworld.com